The Turner E.A.G.L.E. Technique

Order this book online at www.trafford.com
or email orders@trafford.com

Most Trafford titles are also available at major online book retailers.

Edited by: Patricia A. Dingle, Ph.D.
Cover Design by: Pat Dingle
Designed by: Pat Dingle

Printed in United States of America.

ISBN: 978-1-4251-2135-8 (sc)

Library of Congress Control Number: 2010903773

Trafford rev: 04/20/2011

www.trafford.com

North America & international
toll-free: 1 888 232 4444 (USA & Canada)
phone: 250 383 6864 ♦ fax: 812 355 4082
email: info@trafford.com

The Turner E.A.G.L.E. Technique For Incarnation Centered Spirituality:

A Five-Fold Path To Spiritual Wholeness

Rev. Lee W. Turner, Th.D.

Trafford
PUBLISHING

For My Grandchildren
Jeffery, Jamere, Jourdan, and to all Children
becoming spiritual Masters in this generation.

ACKNOWLEDGMENT

I want to acknowledge and express my gratitude to the officers and members of the Greater New Mount Zion Missionary Baptist Church, for their patience in allowing me the time to write this book. I greatly appreciate your encouragement and generous spiritual support. A special thank you is also extended to Dr. Patricia Ann Dingle, for her gracious editorial assistance in this monumental effort, to share the Incarnation of Jesus Christ with God's people. This book would not have been possible without your magnanimous support.

Contents

Path I

Via Positiva, Embracing the Incarnation

Path II

Via Negativa, Controlling the Affection

Path III

Via Creativa, Using Your Generative Powers

Path V

Via Communitiva, Enlightenment for the Beloved Community

PREFACE

In this book I ventured to think through the implications of how a strong spiritual discipline of the Christian religion centered on the Incarnation of Jesus, the Resurrected Lord and being Christian, could empower oppressed African Americans, to overcome the social and political conditions under which they struggle. In this sense, Negro Spirituals and the life of Jesus, as expressed in the history of the Black Experience in this country, shape the spiritual discipline of this book.

I have written this book for the younger generation, ages 15 to 35, and those who like me, find social and political injustices in every area of their lives perpetrated by the majority of the population, who call themselves Christian, both shameful and absolutely appalling. Calling oneself a Christian these days, is an open invitation to a religion that means little more than a social contract to form strong rightwing or leftwing organizations. These organizations in turn build walls to prevent the population of color from enjoying freedom, justice, and identity in this society.

Now is the time for us to develop spirituality that is a response of human freedom, justice, and identity through the Holy Spirit of God. It is time to look for wholeness in the resurrected LORD as a living presence in this present moment. This is the caliber of spiritual discipline that we must develop. But how can such a spiritual discipline in Jesus be developed? Is there a method that can help us to move beyond the historical idea of the Incarnation to the historical person of the Incarnation?

In The Turner E.A.G.L.E. Technique: I layout a plan that presents a process of inner personal spiritual development. This spiritual discipline or development, leads to the spiritual wholeness of the African American believer through a process in which the Incarnation of Jesus and Negro Spirituals are the focal points. The Negro Spirituals, in particular were created by enslaved Africans, struggling to exist in this country. The Negro Spiritual represents their expression of the Christian religion which in turn led to their spiritual wholeness under conditions of abominable slavery and social and political oppression. I do not claim that this book is the only useful spiritual method to meet this important need, but instead it is presented as a way that may engender an appreciation for a strong effort through this book to inspire my people to look for positive methods to transcend the present conditions of our communities.

Lee W. Turner Th. D.
Greater New Mount Zion
Missionary Baptist Church
November 30, 2007

FOREWORD

How can a broken spirit be healed in a broken world? Pastor Lee W. Turner focuses squarely on this question in his first book, *The Turner E.A.GL.E. Technique: A Five-Fold Path to Spiritual Wholeness.*

Turner's book is a heartfelt letter to the Beloved Community of African Americans set against a backdrop of Negro Spirituals. The book beckons the African American Community to transcend from its brokenness in a broken world to a state of spiritual wholeness. Turner guides the reader through his five paths to spiritual healing.

The words of Pastor Turner are timeless. The reader will find his writing both soothing and spiritually-minded. Turner's writing is poignant, honest and straight to the point. As stated earlier, his words are timeless. As the reader reflects on thoughts that have been shared in the book, the reader becomes quiet with anticipation as every page is read. Moreover, when reading *The Turner E.A.G.L.E Technique*, the reader will become so engaged that the reader will become mesmerized by the words such that he or she will feel suspended in time. *The Turner E.A.G.L.E. Technique* will serve to uplift your spirit and put you on the right path.

Turner demonstrates that a whole people can become more adept in serving the Beloved Community and God. With this collective adeptness, each community member can work toward the further development of the Beloved Community where all are valued and every whole person is at one with Almighty God.

Patricia A. Dingle, Ph.D.
Abiding Faith Ministries
Competitive Educational Consulting

INTRODUCTION

I know that young African Americans, between the ages of 15 to 50, are struggling with circumstances in this society, such as racial injustice, and disrespect as an African American person, by those who hold the White supremacy attitude prevalent in our society. I grieve watching you struggle without powerful strategies to meet and positively overcome your experiences in life. I want to help you. I want to help you regain the freedom to dream; I want to help you demand from life the economic justice and judicial justice most often denied you in this society. I want to help you deal with your identity, the real person in your African American skin. You have the right to define who you are as a person. I want you to regain the ability to connect to your history as an African American, as well as, to your ability to reject the history that other people have written about African Americans, which neglects the details of how African Americans persevered through the worse kinds of violence that could be put upon any people. I want you to be able to overcome your difficulties just as your ancestors were able to overcome the slavery, segregation, injustice, and violence they faced daily. I want to help you to rediscover your ancestors' survival strategies.

You must begin by understanding that the most essential strategy for determining the character, culture, unique identity, and ultimate survival of African Americans or Black Americans in this nation is the practice of Black Spirituality. Black Spirituality is an Incarnation Centered Spirituality revealed in the Negro Spiritual. The spirituals are songs drawn straight from the Bible. Long before the Jubilee Singers of Fisk University introduced the Negro Spirituals from 1871 to 1875 to the public, your enslaved ancestors interpreted the Bible in such a way that they found strategies to seek for their own freedom, justice, and identity. They were interpreting the Bible for a spiritual understanding of a freedom that was different from what they heard from the slave masters' preachers. They looked for a freedom from chains and shackles on the plantation, but more significantly, they mainly looked for a freedom to be able to think independently. They also, read the Bible for a meaning of justice that was unlike the master's idea of justice they saw in the slavery system in which they lived. Moreover, the enslaved African American used the Bible to establish an identity as a person other than as a slave or as

chattel property. These enslaved singers of Negro Spirituals rejected any interpretation of the Bible that their masters' preachers tried to teach. Biblical interpretations that the slave masters and their preachers gave were of a kind that told slaves to obey their masters, work hard and they might earn their right to go to heaven when they died.

Today as young African Americans living in this century, you ought to be planning your life's journey. Your purpose for reading this book should be to help you plan your journey for this century. Young African Americans must deal with the fact that the larger community views aspects of African American heritage negatively, intelligence, morality, etc. At this time in your history, your most vital decision should include the determination to return to your deeply implanted spiritual values instilled by your ancestors. These spiritual values enabled your ancestors to survive the most horrific holocaust of African slavery and its aftermath in this nation. We need not apologize for our unique spiritual legacy. See yourselves not as victims because you live as African Americans in a racist society, but see yourselves as victorious survivors of a vicious system.

Your most important act in this century consists of your rediscovery of this most important spiritual legacy. Incarnation Centered Spirituality must be lived. It has the potential to teach you how to practice Incarnation Centered Spirituality as a Black Spirituality. A few dedicated souls continue to live and teach Black Spirituality, but many have almost forgotten this vital practice. Embedded deeply in this ageless spirituality is the real meaning for life and work of your African American enslaved ancestors, just waiting for you to rediscover its powerful strategies. The discovery of this Black Spirituality in a slave-holding society, where slaves lived and survived for years, is vital to your own survival. This slavery system of Western tradition still lives. Slavery of indigenous peoples in Western culture is still shaped by a White supremacy consciousness, not easily ignored nor resisted. The slave-holding mentality and disregard of the worth of African Americans, in this society, is not something that will go away just because wars, marches, and legal edicts have come and gone. This system, still, influences our daily lives. Many African Americans fall prey to its deadly blow as evident in the present status of the broken African American communities within the inner cities and suburbs.

Here is a technique to assist in your journey to wholeness. Wholeness requires the harmonious unification of body, soul, and spirit to accomplish your goals in life, in a way that permits you to meet your needs without preventing others from meeting their needs. The Turner E.A.G.L.E. Technique developed in this book recaptures the powerful method of African American soul survival. The E.A.G.L.E. in The Turner E.A.G.L.E. Technique represents an acronym of Embrace, Affect, Generate, Life, and Enlighten. The Turner E.A.G.L.E. Technique creates a spiritual journey to wholeness. The five elements of the technique explain how to practice Incarnation Centered Spirituality. This spirituality is about learning to live a life of Jesus, a return to your center. Your center consists of your inner self where you meet God. By inner self and interior self it is meant true self. We all need to return to our center. It is in our center where we will find our true self, which helps each of us to become a whole person again. The practice of this spiritual journey demands a five-fold path that takes you to your center of inner self.

We have forgotten how to exercise spiritual discipline. Thus, this method to overcome the tendency for instant gratification and to move beyond shallow living into a deeper level, takes you to your center. Spiritual discipline remains essential to living out the gospel. Spiritual disciplines lived and recommended by all the devotional masters fill many books. The Turner E.A.G.L.E. Technique takes the reader on an inward journey. This book is different from other books of its kind. It shows how to practice New Testament truths that result in personal wholeness while remaining practical. It addresses dualistic thinking.

Dualistic thinking, the double-mindedness, of trying to serve both God and material wealth, presents a 21st century problem for African Americans. Dualistic thinking keeps you conflicted between contrary ideas such as right and wrong, good and bad, white and black. This dualism leaves you unable to think in terms of single-minded solutions. Dualistic thinking lands many in jails, and leads many to lose jobs, to inability to pass standardized tests, to lack of cooperating as a community, and to broken families. Broken lives appear all around, but you have not pinpointed yet the reasons that these conditions remain a part of your daily experience.

Your 21st century challenge for finding wholeness or for avoiding going deep down into a hole of destruction as a people remains before you. Dualistic thinking leaves you insensitive. This insensitivity presents the greatest problem when it comes to interacting with others. Insensitivity reveals symptoms of your broken self. As long as you remain a broken person, you cannot relate to others with sensitivity. Sensitivity reflects a whole person. Wholeness is a unified self that enables you to relate to others.

Wholeness remains our greatest need as African Americans. As I stated above, we need to regain wholeness, with the same spiritual power as our ancestors. Their spiritual power enabled them to endure their ordeal of slavery, segregation, racism, and violence, and still maintain a positive community. You will return to wholeness when you practice the Turner E.A.G.L.E. Technique. Returning to your wholeness for survival as a whole person consists of following the Turner E.A.G.L.E. Technique along the pathway prescribed in this book. Your regained dignity as African Americans comes in just a few well-disciplined steps. When you follow the paths presented in this book, you will experience spiritual power that will amaze you. This book offers a useful plan for African Americans who want to become whole persons and regain their drive for freedom, justice, and identity.

The foundation of the Incarnation of Jesus within the Turner E.A.G.L.E. Technique makes it a useful resource to develop Christian Spirituality. Too much, of what we call spirituality today, falls too far from traditional Christian faith. Christian Spirituality gave your African American ancestors a spirituality of freedom, justice, and identity to be practiced. In fact, they found a Christian Spirituality unique to African Americans in a system of White supremacy. The Negro Spirituals consist of this unique spirituality. Enslaved African Americans created the Negro Spirituals under most severe circumstances. Moreover, African American slave ancestors came out of slavery, not as broken people, but as people who were able to hold their heads up and sing, "Free at last, free at last, thank God almighty, we are free at last." Anger or hatred did not consume your African Americans ancestors.

The choice to exhibit a whole person requires a connection to our ancestors. In this book, you will learn how to use the tools of the Turner E.A.G.L.E. Technique. You will wake up your passive response to life. A passive response to life is not useful. This kind of response comes from the inability to react with power. The power to take control of circumstances cannot happen in a broken person. In life, the broken person suffers for not positively fighting back. This is what we witness in Black communities today. We see large numbers of broken people too powerless to fight back in a positive way, just sitting around on corners. They just don't have the personal power to fight back. Undisciplined behavior lacks the power to fight back. When broken people do try to fight back, they use such negative methods, which result only in circumstances that contain more negativity.

Undisciplined behavior displayed in much of the African American community today projects another symptom of brokenness. The Turner E.A.G.L.E. Technique grows out of the deep roots in Christian Sanctification. Sanctification presents a possible means for you to become whole. This book teaches you how to use sanctification for your spiritual growth. Sanctification is more that just handclapping, loud music, and dancing. It consists of some of this but much more. Sanctification also, comes with God given wholeness promised in salvation. Jesus saved us in order that we could become whole people. However, you have to do your own work of wholeness. Spiritual discipline for wholeness requires effort. This book shows you how to walk a disciplined path to gain wholeness. Thinking that circumstances prevent you from achieving your wholeness is one of the greatest misunderstandings in the African American community of faith today. Understanding enhances the best efforts in any endeavor.

This book helps you to understand the journey to wholeness; however, you must take the journey to receive the full benefit of the Turner E.A.G.L.E. Technique. The truth for your life consists in taking this journey. It is very important that you understand this fact. Many people fail to achieve wholeness in life. We are even unaware, that we are on a path that leads us to a destination. A path is what you choose or stumble into unaware. You chose the path you want to follow or the path will choose you. Discipline is absolutely required. This reinforces why it is important to understand the art of spiritual discipline. At the conclusion of this book, you will understand the relationship between spiritual discipline and personal wholeness.

The Turner E.A.G.L.E. Technique, as pointed out above, is important in the development of spiritual discipline. The Turner E.A.G.L.E. Technique focuses on five techniques. These techniques are the structure that holds together the five paths that make this journey lead you to wholeness. The first technique of the Turner E.A.G.L.E. Technique is "Embrace"; the second technique is "Affect"; the third technique is "Generate"; the fourth technique is "Life," and the fifth technique is "Enlighten." These techniques are each accompanied by four tools. The tools of the Turner E.A.G.L.E. Technique are the strategies that help develop the techniques on the paths. When you use this book as a manual, you will follow the five paths to personal wholeness. As you can see, E.A.G.L.E. is the acronym for the five techniques of this spiritual discipline. You will find the personal power it takes to change and direct your life with the Turner E.A.G.L.E. Technique.

You can join your ancestors in their E.A.G.L.E. flight over their circumstances. It is very important to look at the path you are on in life. The journey differs from the path. The journey is the destination while the path is the direction. Direction makes all the difference in your life. The Turner E.A.G.L.E. Technique leads to wholeness. The five-fold path of Incarnation Centered Spirituality is the Via Positiva, Via Negativa, Via Creativa, Via Transformativa, and the Via Communitiva. See Glossary at end of book. When you know the path, you know the directions. The destination is the "terminal image" of the journey. The last image, the image of completion, in Incarnation Centered Spirituality is "wholeness." The "instrumental image" is "Incarnation." This instrumental image determines the manner in which "we struggle to shape our lives so that we will be open to God's gifts of His saving presence."[1]

Young African Americans between the ages of 15 to 50 need a new focus. A new focus is the most important thing you can expect from this book. Your mind will stay focused on a path that leads to your personal wholeness. Your wholeness is in the paths. As long as you are on the paths, you will have wholeness. This is how you stay focused. In fact, your loss of focus is one of the ways you will know that you are off the path of wholeness. Wholeness, moreover, is the ability to stay focused. You can expect to stay focused on wholeness by using this book. Developmental growth is an additional benefit that you can expect from this book. When you are following the five paths in this book, you are also developing into a whole person. Your personal development is what makes this book worthwhile.

Power is what you really need in life and power is available. The power that your ancestors had is still available to you. All you have to do is rediscover the same spirituality that they discovered. This is an ageless method. In other words, it is not something that is old school. This book will help you rediscover the spirituality of your ancestors. This spirituality is the same spirituality that Jesus practiced when He was on earth—Incarnation Centered Spirituality. Incarnation Centered Spirituality is, in fact, the spirituality of Jesus. Moreover, this book provides a new paradigm of spirituality that leads to wholeness. Wholeness in the African American experience is the power to positively struggle for freedom, justice, and identity.

Through my writing, I have provided a new paradigm of spirituality that leads to wholeness in the African American Experience. Wholeness in the African American Experience is power. The wholeness of African Americans is the power to overcome the ignorance, greed, and selfishness that keep you bound in your own self-imposed slavery. Power is the African American program of spirituality. Each African American will rediscover his or her wholeness of personal power in Incarnation Centered Spirituality. You will learn a paradigm of spirituality for finding the wholeness you need in life. The Turner E.A.G.L.E. Technique develops the substance and framework for African American wholeness, which is the soul survival for Black people in America today.

Survival is more than existing in the world. Survival is living with power to change the environment in which you live. It is having the ability to live a pattern of wholeness and to create new patterns to meet new times and new circumstances. The time has come for young African Americans to reclaim their freedom, justice, identity, and to live their spirituality. In Chapter 1, we begin by using the technique for Embracing in the Turner E.A.G.L.E. Technique of Incarnation Centered Spirituality, in the Path of the Via Positiva.

PATH I

THE VIA POSITIVA
EMBRACING THE INCARNATION

Chapter 1

Starting with Your Affirmation

Mary had a baby, Yes, Lord! Mary had a baby,
Yes, my Lord: Mary had a baby, Yes, Lord! De
People keep-a comin' an' de train done gone.
What did she name him? Yes, Lord! What did
She name him? Yes, my Lord; what did she
Name him? Yes, Lord; de people keep-a comin'
An' de train done gone. She name him King Jesus,
Yes, Lord! Name him King Jesus, Yes, my Lord;
Name him King Jesus, Yes, Lord!

This Negro spiritual, "Mary Had a Baby," expresses an affirmation of the Incarnation of Jesus. The enslaved African American singers embraced the Incarnation as a way of life. Chapter One and the next three chapters deal with the first E of the acronym E.A.G.L.E. in the Turner E.A.G.L.E. Technique. The first of the five paths to be discussed is Path I or the Path of the Via Positiva. The focus of this path is the technique of Embracing the Incarnation of Jesus Christ. The "E" stands for Embrace. In the Path of the Via Positiva, you totally embrace the Incarnation of Jesus beginning with the tool of your affirmation of the Incarnation. The Negro Spiritual shared earlier expresses an African American affirmation of the Incarnation of Jesus. In the 21st century, we have all but abandoned the spirituality expressed in Negro Spirituals. After the Civil Rights movement, many of us have only a lukewarm relationship with the spirituality of our ancestors. We look for a church that we think will meet our religious needs, but when we find a church, we are still disappointed with it because we continue to experience feelings of emptiness. Perhaps, we still have unclear thoughts about religion. Many of us have substituted a relationship with God for the action of going to church. In this chapter, you will learn how to embrace Incarnation by the tool of Affirmation. You will learn how to use the tool of

Affirmation as the embrace of Incarnation on the Path of the Via Positiva.

You can learn how to use the affirmation to embrace the idea of Incarnation in order to embark upon your own personal journey to Incarnation Centered Spirituality: the Five-fold Path to Spiritual Wholeness. The Path of the Via Positiva is important because of our positive knowledge of the Incarnation. Your spiritual journey starts with your positive ideas about God. Positive thinking about God always affirms positive traits that you can actually know about God. Your positive affirmation about the Incarnation creates a worldview in the true sense of the word: a system that reveals the essence of Incarnation as a continuation of Creation, of the place of humanity, of the devastation of sin, and of the grace of redemption. The Path of the Via Positiva is a way of affirming the joy of Incarnation. It produces a hope of cosmic renewal that reveals freedom, justice, identity, truth, meaning, and a celebration of the Spirit.

The first tool of Affirmation in the Turner E.A.G.L.E. Technique is the embracement of the positive presence of the creative energy of the Incarnation that is already at work in your own life. Your affirmation is a statement such as, "I know the idea of Incarnation in human history reveals the moral and spiritual development of humanity from the earliest times until the coming of Jesus. Moreover, I know that Jesus is the Incarnate Person in human history and that I share in the same power of Incarnation in my life because of the coming of Jesus. Thus, right now, I am experiencing my own deification through my positive sanctification as a child of God by the Holy Spirit." Repeat this statement constantly as a mantra. The mantra is "a means of awakening dormant forces in the soul, so that the soul may be enabled to establish contact with the depth-consciousness and to enter into a wider life and a deeper illumination."[2] It is necessary for you to repeat the mantra until your subconscious mind believes it. This is embracing the positive reality of Incarnation. You must believe this before you can believe the journey you are about to take. Embracing the idea of Incarnation is essential to your spiritual journey to wholeness.

Embracing the reality of Incarnation starts with affirming the truth of Incarnation. Affirmation is more than positive thinking. In fact, it is the initial step for embracing Incarnation Centered Spirituality as your way of life. Beginning with your affirmation of Incarnation is also embracing your own personal journey of Incarnation Centered Spirituality. You assert in the affirmation that the man Jesus is the final goal of Incarnation. Therefore, you must make the affirmation as a whole person. This is why the affirmation must be a holistic choice. It must be the choice of the intellect, the affect, and the will. Penetration is the initial purpose of affirmation. When the whole person makes this affirmation, then the illumination of the affirmation penetrates your whole person. When this happens, you will have a separation unto God, an imputation of Christ as your holiness, the possibility of purification from moral evil, and the ability to conform to the image of Christ. At this point, your pathway to wholeness becomes clearer to you.

Affirmation Produces Clarity

When the vision of your affirmation is clear, then faith works to bring your vision of personal wholeness in a broken world into reality. You need to see your wholeness in the Path of the Via Positiva as you travel along the pathway of your affirmation in order to continue the journey. The objective is your personal wholeness in a broken world. Your act of faith illuminates your vision. Essentially, your affirmation is important for the journey because it illuminates the path. The illumination follows your affirmation of faith. This same illumination becomes part of the affirmation and helps you to better see your vision of wholeness better. Because of your act of faith, an inner light illuminates your vision. The illumination follows your commitment to become the whole person repeated in your affirmation mantra. You need to see the wholeness of your path in order to continue your journey. The affirmation makes your objective vision of wholeness understandable to you. However, your vision of wholeness does not take the place of your faith, but rather your faith produces your vision. Your affirmation is your act of faith. Your vision becomes clearly visible to you because of your first act of faith in making the affirmation. You must make the affirmation.

On the Path of the Via Positiva, you develop a feeling of dissatisfaction with knowing that you are a broken person. This is a good thing! Dissatisfaction must exist before any real vision can work. If there is no real dissatisfaction then your total person cannot begin the journey. Desire for the satisfaction of wholeness makes you move toward your vision. With the presence of dissatisfaction in your life, you will now make the journey based on your clear vision of wholeness. Your desire for wholeness becomes the motivating power behind the journey. This, in fact, is the journey of Incarnation Centered Spirituality. The journey along this Path of the Via Positiva becomes your total behavior. There are four components in your total behavior. The components according to William Glasser in his *Choice Theory* are, "thinking, doing, feeling, and physiology--sickening. All behavior consists of these four components."[3] Even broken people have the four components in their total behavior. It is important that you know that all you can ever do is behave. You are always behaving in order to control your environment. The broken person will usually try to control the environment by behaving with emotions or with physiology, more than with thinking or with acting. The whole person controls the environment by thinking or acting to solve problems. When one approaches, one's problems in life by using intellect, one will also control one's feelings. When one approaches problem solving by acting rationally, one can expect useful results. However, if one tries to solve one's problems by using emotions and/or physiology instead of intellect or thinking, one is in danger of making matters worse. Emotions are not rational. The truth of the matter is that you are in control only as you use your intellect and your actions. The reason that some African Americans end up in so much trouble in this society today is that they try to solve their problems emotionally or by physiology. I am not suggesting that emotions are not useful. Emotions can be a very good barometer for detecting the circumstances of your environment. You should trust your feelings; sometimes feelings are the best protection against negative things in your environment. However, the only thing you can do about the physiology is to take care of your health. Trying to control the environment with your feelings or physiology is a waste of your energy.

The Image of Baby Jesus Fuels Your Imagination

We have seen from the Negro spiritual, "Mary Had a Baby," that African Americans have vital imaginations. The spiritual "Mary had a baby" is a statement of God's greatest imagination. These enslaved singers embraced the imagination of the Creator. The image of Baby Jesus in a manger is an important part of Incarnation Centered Spirituality. The Uniqueness of Jesus, in fact, is his image as the baby in a manger. This image fuels the imagination with mystery, possibilities, and purpose. This image is unique in Incarnation Centered Spirituality because Jesus is the divine human person. Your affirmation, in the first place, is about Jesus of Nazareth the divine human person. His uniqueness makes your total person take notice of Him. Jesus makes one aware of one's own brokenness. Divine humanity is quite an idea for the mind to embrace, especially the divine person as a baby in a manger. Possibilities become visible with the image of Jesus, a child born of a virgin and laid in a manger. Each person needs the vision of the purity of Baby Jesus in order to start the journey of Incarnation Centered Spirituality. The image of Baby Jesus is an image of perfect purity. Purity will always produce humility. Humanity can see the glory of God only after the self has been emptied of worldly desires and carnal thinking. This would include for example, a self-serving ego and excessive pride. In the image of Baby Jesus, the New Birth is possible. This is why the virgin womb is part of your first affirmation. The whole person makes the commitment to embrace the Baby Jesus in a manger. This is the substance of the journey along the Path of Via Positiva. When the commitment is made to Incarnation Centered Spirituality, an objective reality appears in your personal journey to wholeness. You realize your own personal authenticity, which means that you know that you have the right to be whole. As you journey with your affirmation on the Path of the Via Positiva, you realize that the Creator validates you, and you recall that God made you in His own image.

Find Your Own Authenticity

Authentic experience is the only way that you can be who you are supposed to be. There can be no other way. Authenticity is, after all, what you are striving to achieve in life. You cannot achieve genuineness if you do not have the definitive authentic experiences that you are trying to achieve. Spirituality is an attempt to achieve your authenticity. Authenticity is personal wholeness. Personal wholeness makes one a bona fide person. You already have the push and pull of the experience of wholeness in the affirmation. You already embraced wholeness in your affirmation. When you really want to achieve something, you must already sense what you want to achieve in your life. You are trying, in this case, to achieve your personal wholeness in a broken world. The idea of Incarnation, as we have already stated, has a very old history. Incarnation reveals the moral and spiritual development of humanity from the earliest time in history to the coming of Christ. You must understand that the Incarnation is a revelation of the divine mystery in terms that humanity can understand. This revelation goes back even to the time before written history. However, we do know that there is the idea of the Incarnation of Krishna in the Hindu religion. Then there is the Buddha, although a historical person who appears as the ultimate principle of being a revelation of God, nevertheless, is still only an idea of Incarnation in history. On the other hand, the person of Jesus as the Word of God made flesh in history is an experience that makes all the difference in the world. There is a big difference between an idea of Incarnation in history and an actual person of Incarnation in history. This difference is because the person Jesus is historically God in the flesh according to attributes that no other possesses. The Word of God is the eternal wisdom of God revealed to us through the Incarnation of Jesus Christ. In His Incarnation, you have the experience of your own wholeness. Thus, you possess the experience of wholeness in the intellectual affirmation of Incarnation because you used words of Incarnation. The Scripture says, "As he thinks in his heart so is he, [Proverbs 23:7]." You are the sum total of your thoughts. Moreover, the very act of thinking requires you to use words. Therefore, thinking is language. Thus, you must become aware of your use of language. Furthermore, language is the very means of communicating with the Creator. God created you with the idea that you and He would stay in contact by talking together. We call this act of talking with God prayer. Prayer is not one-way communication. God created you to know God. The Path of the Via Positiva is the response to God's call to know Him. Thus, you are able to be a hearer of the Word of God. Transmission of ideas can only occur in language. Conversion happens after the Word of God penetrates the soul. It is important at this point to remember that you must embrace the concept of Incarnation for wholeness in this broken world since this constitutes the beginning of the conversion experience. The knowledge of God's Word presents the possibility of our conversion. However, you remain unconverted until you embrace the concept of Incarnation by faith. Conversion comes when head knowledge becomes heart knowledge. Heart knowledge is the knowledge that already exists in the inner self.

Gnosis is Your Inner Knowledge

You become aware of your inner knowledge because of your affirmation. This inner knowledge is your personal knowledge, the divine knowledge that comes with your natural birth, but more importantly, it is knowledge about your present spiritual journey. You know that you know the spiritual truths of Incarnation in the inner self. This inner knowledge is called gnosis. Essentially, the basic requirement for making a spiritual journey to wholeness is the acceptance of the inner knowledge of the true self. By true self, reference is made to your innermost self. Gnosis is the knowledge in the inner self that enables you to meet this requirement. The inner self is your true self, the ground of your personal being, which is one with God--the eternal Being. The false self is your ego-self, independently seeking to be master of its own world, without knowing the truth, and thereby being cut off from the eternal wisdom of God. The eternal wisdom of God is within your inner self. Moreover, this true self comes alive through the conversion experience. The Word is becoming flesh as your true self.

Gnosis is what you have always had in your true self but you could not experience it because of your false self. Once the true self is alive through conversion, you share the eternal wisdom of God. You can now enter into the divine mystery with the positive knowledge of God. There is a divine mystery in the midst of the profane. This divine mystery is at the Center, the point of contact with God. The Center is the point of Ultimate Reality, the Holy

Ground where heaven and earth meet. Ultimate Reality is the divine mystery towards which you are journeying. There is no other way you can enter into Ultimate Reality without the wisdom of God working in your true self. The wisdom of God working in your true self is essential on the journey to Ultimate Reality.

The true self is receptive to the Wisdom of God. The true self is the unified self, a divine unified quartet of the Trinity and you. This unified foursome is God the Father, Jesus the Son, the Holy Spirit and you united into one person. As a divine unified quartet, faith for you in Jesus Christ, is more than an empty concept. Faith is the force of your life that enables you to do what you do. This is why entering into the divine mystery is necessary. All reality is mystery, but Ultimate Reality is the connection of the holy foursome in the Ground of Being. Some knowledge in the spiritual life eludes us until we have entered into divine mystery. Entering into divine mystery is the same as embracing Incarnation. Entering the divine mystery is like climbing a knotted rope. To begin with, Divine Mystery is about revelation, God's self-disclosure, essentially, embracing Incarnation is encountering the Incarnate Word of God. At this point, you are encountering the revelation of the Eternal Word of God. Revelation is the grease that takes care of the squeaks along the journey of Incarnation Centered Spirituality. You will rediscover gnosis as the original spiritual knowledge in human nature through revelation. Moreover, you learn this eternal truth through God's Word. Scripture validates this truth.

The Scripture calls the Word that personally affects you with truth and knowledge Rhema. There are two important words in the New Testament used to denote Word, one is Logos, which means the expression of thought or an idea. The other word is Rhema, which means the actual utterance in speech or writing. It means, in this case, the individual scripture that the Spirit brings to your remembrance for use at the time you need it. Thus, the Rhema Word is in the Logos Word. Rhema is your personal word that reveals the Will of God to your intellect. The Rhema Word brings faith into your life. The Apostle Paul says, "Faith comes by hearing and hearing by the Rhema of Christ [Roman 10:17]." Without the Rhema Word, there is no other way you can rediscover gnosis. Distinction, as we know, marks one thing apart from another thing. Revelation is that distinction, which comes from your affirmation embracing Incarnation. Revelation is the result of the affirmation. Revelation is illumination. Revelation is a very necessary part of becoming a whole person. The revelation of Incarnation Centered Spirituality gives you insight into your true self; this insight into your true self lets you see the gnosis that distinguishes whole persons from broken persons. The Rhema Word "calling" you to wholeness will always be the calling that distinguishes whole persons from broken persons; the calling is also the light that comes with the Rhema Word. God calls you to original harmony. Embedded in the inner self is a distinct memory of a lost harmony. The memory of a lost harmony will always trouble you until you have the satisfaction of the restored harmony of wholeness.

On the Path of the Via Positiva, you can realize when you have lost the relationship with God because it is evident in your action of turning to untrue gods. However, you cannot fool yourself. You know that false gods are inferior and are not able to give you a lasting satisfaction. For the Image of God, remains active within your true self. Now you have become aware that the Image of God is still active in your inner self. Therefore, the Image of God survived your brokenness and will always survive to reign over your life. Even though you still have a guilty, restless feeling of dissatisfaction, with anything that the rational will collects for you that is not of God. Be aware that the Image of God survives within you both as a guarantee of your possibility of wholeness and as a principle of your discontentment and dissatisfaction with anything that is not of God. Howard Thurman talks about the natural concern that humanity has with the beginnings, with the contemplation concerning origins. Thurman says we examine the "various accounts of this work of origins we are face to face with the memory of a lost harmony."[4] In the Creation story, the beginning of man on earth is orderly, and harmonious, but in actual experience today, there is a strong awareness of disharmony. Yet in Creation, there is memory of harmony. God of Creation remembers and insists on harmony. The Word of God brought Creation into being. God remembers His Word of Creation. Subsequently, Incarnation is the core of Creation and thus the highest purpose of God. Man is created in God's own image. Genesis 2: 26-27 says:

> And God said, Let us make man in our own image, after our likeness; and let them have dominion over the fish of the sea, and over the foul of the air, and over the cattle, and over all the earth, and over every creeping thing that creepeth upon the earth. So God created man in his own image, in the image of God created he him; male and female created he them.

Humanity has a memory of a harmony that continues to inform the inner self that man is an Incarnation of the likeness and Image of God according to God's Word. We all need answers to questions raised by the concept of Incarnation embedded in our collective inner self. Who am I? Why am I here?

What is my purpose in life? How do I find meaning for my life? Why am I dissatisfied with the way I am? These questions haunt the memory. Having these questions within our inner self always unsettles us.

There is a memory of the Incarnation in your inner self that will not let you rest. Our knowledge of Incarnation within our inner self constantly reminds us of the lost harmony, this concept again remains deeply implanted in our true self. Man is, even in the broken state, still the Incarnation of the Image of God. This is why down through history humanity has looked for the Incarnation of a Savior. As we have said, the concept of Incarnation predates Judeo-Christian scriptures. There has always been the idea of a Divine Savior coming into human history to save broken humanity. However, you have found your Incarnate Savior in the person of Jesus. In His Incarnation, you find a divine capacity to rediscover God in your inner self.

Rediscovering God

Keep in mind, your affirmation of Incarnation results in your capacity to rediscover God. You are born with the capacity to rediscover God in your true self. Until the New Birth, you lived in your false self. Many things called you to rediscover God in your life. Unfortunately, you were so preoccupied with discovering other things that you never got around to rediscovering God. God calls us in many ways. Beauty often calls us to the idea of God many times but we think in terms of aesthetics instead of in terms of divinity. This level of thinking takes us away from knowledge of God until we learn again that beauty is part of divinity. Truth evades us until we come into the knowledge that truth, beauty, and divinity are all one in the same thing. The difference in this way of thinking is the conscious level upon which you regularly function. There is a level of consciousness in all life, which is in some degree of development; of all the forms of life on earth, man has the highest degree of consciousness development. Even sounds and shapes articulate truth to our unified human intelligence. Observe how this unified intelligence enables you to rediscover God in a clear way. Truth becomes real only when it pierces your heart.

Many of you think of the heart as a mechanical pump distributing blood throughout the body. Biologically speaking this is a fact. However, in the sense of spirituality, the heart is the core of your very being. The center of being is where and how you connect with God. The Image of God is the spark of divinity in the heart where you make connection with God. This spark of divinity ignites the heart with spiritual energy. The divine spark influences you from the center of your being. The spiritual center of your being also contains the intention of God. When you stop and think about the center of your being, you soon learn that there is only one center. There is a concentric field of influence that flows from your center. Eric Butterworth makes the point that you have a center. He makes it clear that there is a spiritual point in the "center where God becomes you."[5] Now understand this is a point of changeless oneness. God is the center of the universe. God stays at the center. However, universal center is everywhere--at the center of the being where God's Spirit energizes Creation, the divine spark, and God's intention. When God's Spirit energizes Creation, God, also energizes the divine life. Divine energy flows from the Godhead. In biology, we learn that life will always have five basic characteristics which distinguish life from non-life.

You Can Understand the Five Characteristics of Life

We learn from biological science that five specific characteristics indicate life. Life manifests itself through five abilities that inanimate objects do not possess. Life has abilities of (1) reproduction, (2) growth from within, (3) response to stimuli, (4) metabolism, and (5) movement. These same abilities are true of Spiritual Life. Henry Drummond points out that there is a "Law of Continuity, a Law of laws."[6] According to this Law of Continuity, Laws of natural life must be those of spiritual life, as below so above, the same five characteristics of natural life apply also to spiritual life. Be alert to this fact; when Incarnation illuminates us, an internal fire starts burning. Also, expect, the Word of God to ignite the spark of divinity in the inner self, where you responded by faith. The Divine Spark makes you alive with new birth. When this happens, the true self has ability to walk the path of Incarnation Centered Spirituality as supernatural life with the same five abilities as biological life.

As long as we are obedient to God's Word, we remain whole with supernatural life. Responsibility becomes the by-word for obtaining Supernatural Life. This is divine life of the New Birth in Christ. Divine life comes with Jesus. It is important that you recognize New Birth as the continuation of Creation in the Incarnation of Jesus. God is the Creator of this new life in Jesus Christ. Consequently, you have the same life Adam had before he became a broken person through his disobedience. You are responsible for receiving the New Birth through faith and for living in the New Birth by obedience. Responsibility is meeting your needs without preventing others from meeting their needs.

Come Alive With Supernatural Life

Each person must take responsibility for meeting the need to come alive with supernatural life given through the Incarnation of Jesus. This personal responsibility modifies the idea of a universal salvation. Salvation is the path to supernatural life. It is a personal choice. Salvation operates in life as the only means to experience the divinity. Nevertheless, God is Spirit and we must approach God in spirit and in truth. God is eternal. God is in you and you are in God. A human being lives beyond simple existence. Too many people think just eating, sleeping, and making love is good enough. Many people only want to do what they call just getting by. However, the "being" in human being, means the possession of a potential for supernatural life. They have a potential power for wholeness. We regain personal wholeness by regaining spiritual power in a broken world through supernatural life. Embracing Incarnation with affirmation leads to an awakening of spiritual growth that comes with a new worldview. In Chapter 2, you will learn how to use the tool of awakening to a new worldview in the Path of the Via Positiva. You learn also, what it means to be an awakened person in a sleepwalking world.

Chapter 2

Awakening from Your
Self-Imposed Hypnosis

Go tell it on the mountain,
Over the hills and everywhere;
Go tell it on the mountain,
That Jesus Christ is born.

The Path of the Via Positiva in the pathway of awakening is the breakthrough.
The enslaved singers of this spiritual, "Go Tell It On The Mountain" possessed a wide awakened inner self. They broke out of their self-imposed hypnosis. The Incarnation of Jesus excited them with an expectation of a New
Birth of freedom, of justice, and of identity. These enslaved singers received an
awakening to a New Birth of the historical Jesus. Moreover, their own awakening to an historical Jesus follows the affirmation of Incarnation. The above
spiritual, reveals what African Americans thought about the Incarnation of
Jesus. The above spiritual also expresses an awareness of the historical Jesus.
We have always taken for granted the reality of the historical Jesus as well
as the Christ of faith. However, after the Civil Rights movement, we went
to sleep in regard to the Incarnation of the historical Jesus. You must now
awaken from your self-imposed hypnosis. When you embraced the idea of
Incarnation with determination to make the spiritual journey of wholeness,
your consciousness moved to a level of awareness that makes you want to go
tell the Incarnation of Jesus on the mountain and everywhere. You were asleep
before you made the affirmation. We know you thought you were awake.
However, you were truly asleep. You chose to be asleep because you thought
it best not to be aware of too much around you. You convinced yourself that
you could do nothing about your pain and suffering in life. Consequently, you
developed a lifestyle of being unaware in order not to deal with the painful
things you saw in life. As you choose to be in a state of self-hypnosis, you are
robbing your self of an exciting life. Try to understand that the Creator or-

dered your life. You have decided to reorder your own life by being unaware of the painful things in your environment. It is time that you learn there is something much better in life for you than being a sleepwalker. You are in a self-induced hypnotic state. Embracing Incarnation takes you to another level of consciousness beyond self-induced hypnosis. It makes you become awakened to your true self

The Hypnosis is Self-induced

Understand that all hypnosis is self-induced. Embracing Incarnation truly results in your awakening out of self-induced hypnosis. The awakening is the act of snapping out of the state of self-induced hypnosis. Therefore, you see, it is possible that you are unaware that you are hypnotized. This is why snapping out of hypnosis is a form of awakening out of sleep. Your awakening is making contact with a new sense of reality. It is helpful to know that contacting new reality is making new connections with reality. New reality is always present. Nevertheless, only when we awaken to reality is contact with new reality possible. Many of us are daily walking around half conscious of our environment. You continue to do what you have always been doing. You even believe what you are doing is the only way to do what you are doing. Becoming aware that there is another way to see and do things is what it means to snap out of self-induced hypnosis. There is no way you will or can ever snap out of a state of mind that you are not even conscious of being in, until you admit that there is more to life than you are aware. The tool of awakening is for your becoming a whole person. It is to help you to awaken to your own self-induced hypnosis. It is only by raising your consciousness that you will become aware of the environment. This is why the raising of consciousness is a growing spirituality. You have the capacity to raise your consciousness. Furthermore, human consciousness is capable of limitless expansion. Start believing that you can reach a height of consciousness you never thought you could reach. You must move beyond the point of awareness where you are right now in life. There is a range of extension for everything in Creation. If you watch the growth of a plant in a high-speed camera, you can see the plant extending to its limit. When there is no extension beyond where we are in a given time, there is no growth. Let yourself believe that extended consciousness is important. It is important to be awake in life. It is only by your state of consciousness that you know how awake you really are in life. Therefore, you can snap out of self-induced hypnosis when you are ready to extend your consciousness. Start by realizing that the Incarnation of Jesus is the beginning of the New Birth. The New Birth in Christ is your initial extension of consciousness. This reality changed the consciousness of history for most of us; on planet earth, we speak of calendar years as B.C. and A.D. The New Birth is certainly the beginning of a new spiritual growth. From the time of the New Birth, you have the ability to awaken your own self from sleep. You can continue your New Birth by raising your consciousness.

You Should Continue Your Birth Process

All physical birth is a continuous process of growth and development. Birth moves toward a new awareness of existence. Even the fetus in a mother's womb is aware of its existence. As the birth process continues your awareness continues. Therefore, you should never forget that even physically you are in a birthing process of eternity. Intervention moves the process forward. Realize that every event in the life can be an intervention for both physical and spiritual growth. Even the meeting of the sperm and egg is an intervention in the process of growth. Moreover, pain is intervention. Pain is a catalyst that moves the process toward full existence of being. This is why a new level of awareness of spiritual existence along the path of the Via Positiva is both possible and necessary. In the Path of the Via Positiva, the tool of Awakening is full of interventions. Growth is always painful. Pain is really, the reason why many do not want to grow. It hurts to grow. Growth is physically and psychologically painful. Pain is useful for the journey. Remaining aware of pain is how you continue the New Birth process. In this case, no pain no gain is true. Significantly, somewhere along the path with the tool of Awakening you will become exhausted. Be particularly aware here that the feeling of exhaustion always acts as an alert to you that it is necessary for you to make a change in your life. Exhaustion is also an intervening opportunity for growth and development. For example when a baby is exhausted from crawling it starts walking.

Exhaustion is that point we reach when we have come to the end of a level of maturity in life. Your life will have run its course at this point of exhaustion. Start telling yourself that you are ready for a new experience when this happens. Exhaustion creates emptiness in life. The desire for something different in your life makes itself felt at this point. This happens when you have come to the point in life where you realize that there is more to life than what you have. You are tired of the same old thing. Exhaustion is your internal wake-up call. When you desire something different, it is because you are aware that something different is possible, and that something is missing in your life. Expansion of awareness is otherwise impossible without this exhaustion. There can be no expansion until there is room for expansion.

After you, reach conscious awareness of meaning in life there is new room for meaning in your life. Life will have lost its meaning for you until you become aware of a new purpose, a new word, and thus a new meaning for being. Spiritual growth is expansion of consciousness. When you reach a level of disillusionment, you become awakened to a spiritual need. You sense a permanency in Creation that has heretofore evaded your consciousness.

Stay Alert to Your Sense of Permanency

As you grow spiritually, you sense the permanency of your nature. Although you may be unaware of permanency in your life, permanency exists in your nature. With your nature of permanency, your sense of need for unity, and your sense of need for completion in this world, you will always have a feeling of disillusionment in life. You need to be awakened to this element of disillusionment. It is the origin of your spiritual growth process. This spiritual growth process began with your embrace of the Incarnation. This spiritual growth leads to awaken you to disillusionment in your life. Embrace this disillusionment. There is a law of disillusionment at work in the spiritual life. We are of a permanent nature yet in our own lives, we experience impermanency. Arthur Chandler in his book, *An Essay In Mystical Theology* helped me to understand this "law of disillusionment"[7] that is at work in our spiritual life when our demand for permanence is not met. You see we have a permanent nature that will not let us be content with what is basically transitory. This is why the world can never give us lasting satisfaction. You must be alert in order to deal with this demand for permanency to achieve fulfillment in this life. We are restless when we sense we have only temporary parts of the world, things that are passing away while we have a permanent nature. You have flashing incidents of awareness that things in the world are only temporary.

Therefore, your permanent nature makes you aware that temporary things will not give you a lasting satisfaction. You must awaken to the fact that there is a need for unity in your life. Your nature is a complex unity of intellect, emotion, and will. Therefore, that which will satisfy you must be a complete unity that is able to meet the needs of the variety of interests in your nature. You know that you cannot have your cake and eat it too. So you look for that single experience which will draw all the different experiences into a unified whole. This is why disillusionment on the Path of the Via Positiva is always part of your growth experience. Remember that on the Path of the Via Positiva this spiritual growth process of disillusionment is also part of your embrace of Incarnation. The Path of the Via Positiva shines the tool of awareness in your inner self. We turn to religion. Religion is our effort to answer the needs of our permanent nature in a changing world. This is why you need to understand that Jesus gave us something more than religion, He gave us God. God lights our path of awakening even to reveal our disillusionments.

Let His Light Shine

The light of God is inspiration from God. Be aware of the light of God. It is your inspiration in your inner self. The inspiring light of God opens your inner eye to a positive way of seeing human significance and divine presence in your inner self. This inspiration comes as a new impulse of light. Be awakened to the truth that God puts divine light in the inner self. This is the divine intention that God puts in the inner self for growth. This intention is the spark of divinity. Sometimes it comes through as idea bursting into your consciousness. This idea is most likely God's intention for your life. This spark is the intention of God illuminating your inner self with divine light. The remarkable thing about this divine intention is that it is God's will at work in the whole Creation. Keep in mind that you are part of Creation governed by the same intentions of God as all Creation. Divine intention moves all Creation in the direction God intends. Remember, it is God's divine intention through His Word that created humanity. God continues the creation process through His Word.

In the Old Testament, the Word "Dabhar" is the divine creative energy of God. In the Old and New Testaments, the Word of God speaks to humanity as a continuing act of Creation. However, there is the word "Rhema" in the New Testament that you should remember. Be awakened to the Rhema Word. The Rhema Word is the Word of God in the New Testament that talks to us in this life. The Rhema Word keeps us informed about what God is doing in our lives and moves us towards divinity. In the Path of the Via Positiva, you will become awakened to the Rhema Word of God in a new way. The flash of light in your soul is the Rhema Intention of God that becomes the inspiration, the intention, and the wisdom. Stay awake to the Rhema Word of God. The Rhema Word of God flows out from God but remains in God! The flowing Word of God is the positive dimension of Incarnation Centered Spirituality. The Word of God is eternal.

Eternity Influences You in Time

Grasp an awakening in a sense of eternity. Eternity is an imposing, intruding truth. There is always imposing truth of eternity in life making us aware of it in spite of what we do. Eternality is initial truth. "In the beginning was the Word and the Word was God" is a statement of initial truth. Therefore, the eternal structure upon which everything stands is the foundational of initial truth. If we dig deep enough into life, we will discover this eternal truth upon which the whole structure of Creation is standing. When we ignore this foundation, our spiritual structure is in danger of falling and losing its purpose. This, in fact, is the judgment for being unaware of foundational truth. Judgment is possible only because there is an eternal foundational truth. It is always good to view this imposing truth as the best thing God has put in Creation. This imposing truth holds the universe on course. It is what makes science possible. It keeps flashing in your inner self. It is a continuous infusion for good in your life. This truth is always trying to awaken you out of your hypnotic sleep. However, you do not want to wake up. You like your hypnotic sleep even though you are having nightmares. This is evidence you can see on any street in the African American Community. On the other hand, there is an awesome experience waiting for your awakened inner self. You awaken by coming out of the darkness and going into the light. The best way to shake a person out of sleep is to turn on the light.

A flash of eternity is awesome. Understand that the experience of awesomeness is more than just a striking fancy. It is the attention getter that makes you stop and consider the wonders of Creation and the Creator. Stop and look around at the Creation. If there were no such thing as awesomeness, you would have no reason to awaken yourself from your sleep. Notice that I said awaken your self. This is a foundational truth. Only you can awaken yourself out of your sleep. Therefore, the awesomeness of perfection alerts you of your own need for perfection. The Image of God in you shows up as faith in the ideal of perfection. But the world is unable to satisfy this need for perfection. This leaves us with a sense of disillusionment that again sends us back to God. Significantly, the need for perfection is awesome. Perfection has the ability to inspire a sense of awe in your inner self. We all are stopped in our tracks when we experience the need for perfection. It intrudes into our sleepwalking. Moreover, perfection is not only awesome but it is also demanding. Therefore, it is an intervention of eternity. Because we sense that there is a need for perfection, in our world, in our being, we can never rest with imperfection even if we try to ignore it we are aware of it. Much of your sleepwalking is your effort to ignore imperfection in the world. Imperfection eats away at our senses until we react to it.

We cannot ignore imperfection forever. There is, as we have said, the memory of a lost harmony that will not let us ignore the beauty of perfection that floods our souls and leaves us speechless. This flash of eternity will awaken us out of our sleep and guide us on our journey to wholeness. We have to be alert enough to embrace the flash of the eternity of harmony. It is there, even though, we try to hide from it in our sleep. Remember, the old Negro spiritual says, "There is no hiding place down here." This is an eternal truth. In fact, spirituality means awakening to the growth process that alerts us to the fact that there is no hiding place down here. This fact drives the continuous expansion of divine intention in our inner self. It awakens our compassion for the Creation.

When You Are Awake You Care

When you care for others, you are awake. To be awake is to have a sense of otherness. Otherness is an experience that makes us know that there must be a heaven somewhere. If there were no heaven then, we would invent one. Stay awake to the fact that if we could invent heaven, heaven must be there already or we would not know what to invent. Using the tool of awakening, we sense that heaven is our destiny. This sense of destination makes us know that we are always on our way to a better place. The thought of going to a place better than this place would be a delusion if there were no heaven. The awakened self knows that God does not lead us into delusions. If it is possible to continue on a path to something worse or a path to something better, then it is logically possible to go to hell or to heaven. Since we have this sense of heaven, it would also be irrational if hell does not exist. This is not double thinking. Heaven and hell constitute one path to you, just different directions. However, you must always have a sense of heaven and hell in order for you to have a balanced center. Your sense of perfection makes it necessary that there must be a heaven as well as a hell. You need a real sense of heaven in order to stay awake. However, in the Path of the Via Positiva, there can never be a time when there is no sense of heaven. The Via Positiva is a positive reality of Creation and the Creator. Humanity always sensed a heaven and hell in one form or another. You must awaken to unified possibilities of heaven and hell as a present reality. Nevertheless, you must recognize that the tool of awakening must always go in a direction towards heaven or a direction away from hell.

Having a Sense of Beyond Keeps You Awake

Your sense of heaven will keep you awake. Heaven is always beyond. Being aware of the beyond is to be awake. When you keep, your focus in life beyond where you are in life you will stay awake. Beyond is that place toward which your awakened mind is always moving. Thinking about the beyond is how your mind opens and upgrades itself. Renewal of your mind would otherwise not happen without the pull on your mind towards the beyond. Beyond does not necessarily mean a sense of up there, because in the universe there is no such thing as up there. In order to have an up there, you must also presuppose fixed points of reference. No fixed point in the spiritual life other than Jesus exists. God cannot serve as a fixed point. In fact, nothing in the universe can be considered a fixed point that could indicate an up there. Even when we talk about the earth as a fixed point, we still must be aware that space ships go out into space instead of up into space. This is important because our minds open only when we recognize that earth must never be a fixed point to have an opened and upgraded mind. An opened and upgraded mind is an awakened mind. Your awakened mind is in a receptive mode of prayer.

You must understand that your awakened state is your act of prayer. Prayer is the vocation of the spiritual traveler. Therefore, prayer is your vocation. If you are awake to the will of God, you will have to be receptive to the voice of God. This is how a receptive mode of mind operates with an awakened mind. Expectation, remember, whatever you do, is always prayer. There is no reason to pray if there is no expectation. Change comes when there is expectation. Hence, you must stay awake with expectations. Without expectations, changes always catch us by surprise, as if we are asleep. When you have no expectations, you are always reacting to change instead of being proactive to change. Moreover, the reaction to change is always hostility. A receptive mode of mind operates with awakening because your mind is receptive. It pays to have a prayer life that is both receptive and expecting. Your prayer life will make the change in your life a positive experience. Your experiences will be expectations that meet your desires.

Remember desire, as we have seen, is your inner fire that ignites your motivation in life. Desire is an expectant mode of mind that can be positive or negative for your journey. It is very necessary for you to be alert to your desires. Many things can cause us to become active but nothing causes us to be motivated faster than desire. Desire is the force that puts a sizzling fire in your soul and ignites your passions. Desire is the fuel that keeps us active. However, being asleep extinguishes the fire. You must become awakened to your desires! Desire is more powerful than you realize.

Your Awareness Permits Your Transcendence

As your consciousness extends, you can transcend your circumstances in life. Transcendence is possible only when you are aware of your location, when you understand what it takes to move forward, and when you know your direction. This takes a fully alert mind. Stay awake to the possibilities of transcendence by being aware of the path that you are on. When you are aware of the path, you can overcome the obstacles blocking your path. Think about rising beyond whatever is blocking your progress. Awareness makes transcendence possible in life. When you become aware of where you are, you begin seeking ways to rise beyond the negative places. When you are awake, your understanding increases as you realize what your circumstances are. Understanding, in fact, is the beginning of transcendence. The trouble is that most of us would rather go down to the pits than to awake from our sleep. Wake up! Your direction becomes plain when you desire another place in life. A clear knowledge of directions is always necessary for transcendence. You can never know where you should go until you know your direction and you can never know your direction until you know where you should go. It all starts with being awake to your present location. Let yourself awake to discover where you are in life. Awakening to the Lamb of God is to focus on your journey.

In Incarnation Centered Spirituality, you must behold the Lamb of God. The Baby Jesus is the Lamb of God. You simply must remain aware of the Lamb of God. The Lamb of God is the trailblazer. He is the Word of God. Moreover, the Word of God produces faith. Faith is awareness. Faith is the only way that beholding the Lamb of God is possible. Therefore, it is essential for you to behold the Lamb of God, if you are to know that you are awakened from your self-induced hypnosis. The Lamb of God is the awakening source of your ability to travel the path using the tool of Awakening in Incarnation Centered Spirituality. The Lamb of God is the source of what the Christian spiritual life is supposed to be. We can never know what spiritual life is supposed to be until we behold the Lamb of God. Grace is the gift of God that lets you become aware of the possibilities of beholding the Lamb of God. Grace comes to us as the Gift of God in life and imparts faith to trust the knowledge that there is a source of spiritual life in the Lamb of God. Truth is the light that makes your path bright enough to see both the Lamb of God and to see where you are walking. Sleepwalking causes you to miss this important source.

Your Goal is the Personality of Jesus

The most important thing you must be awake to is that your goal is to become like Jesus. Your awakened mind knows that Jesus is the Lamb of God, whom we embraced as the Baby Jesus for wholeness. Wholeness becomes personal to us only when Jesus becomes real to us on another level. Healing is a necessary part of becoming whole in a broken world. Jesus comes still with healing in his hands. Jesus became human in order that we might become divine. He is also your source of divinity. In Chapter 3, you will learn how to relate to Jesus Christ as your reminder of what it means to be a child of God. You will learn that Jesus is the Word of God calling us to become Words of God as the continuation of the Incarnation. You will also learn how to use the tool of the best human model to imitate for the purpose of advancing your own spiritual growth.

Chapter 3

Finding the Best Human Model

Give me Jesus, give me Jesus,
you may have all dis worl', give
me Jesus, Oh, Give me Jesus. Give
me Jesus, give me Jesus, You may have
all dis worl' give me Jesus.

African Americans have always had a strong desire for Jesus as the spiritual, "Give Me Jesus" expresses. We have always sensed that Jesus is our best model of what it means to be God's child. We embrace the truth that Jesus is the Incarnate Son of God who became man, died on a cross, and experienced the resurrection from the dead. Moreover, we awaken to the truth that Jesus provides the only source for our wholeness. Jesus as the source of our personal wholeness creates a new reality for us in African American history. It is your new possibility as an African American for a relationship with your Creator. The Incarnation of Jesus provides an enabling ability to connect to a divine force that is already present in your innermost self. At first, you embraced the idea of Incarnation in history, but now you embrace Jesus, the Incarnate Person in history. You affirm Jesus as your Savior and as your reminder of what it means to be God's child. You have now come from embracing the idea of Incarnation in history to embracing the person of Incarnation in history, as your source of personal wholeness. Jesus is the Divine Son of God who is now your best human model for living as a child of God. His coming produced a new form of grace in history. This grace makes it possible for you to enter into a new relationship with God in history as the Father. The grace of God comes with the Incarnation of Jesus in a new way. The scripture says it this way, "For the law was given by Moses, but grace and truth came by Jesus Christ [John 1:17]." This is the same grace of God the Father. God's grace is always God's grace. In other words, this is God's old grace but with new possibilities. The coming of Jesus brings the possibility of living with a new kind of life with God in a different way. The greatest part of the Incarnation of Jesus is the role He played in our salvation, by taking our sins upon Himself and dying on the cross as the sacrificial lamb for the atonement of sin. The important thing about the word atonement is that it is an Old Testament word meaning covering sin according to the Mosaic Law. However, in the New Testament, there is a vital contrast between "covered" and "taken away." Therefore, the word *atonement* does not apply in the New Testament. The word atonement is mentioned here in order to emphasize the developmental process of the grace of God. The grace of God as the Atonement is 'at-one-meant': those once on bad terms with God can come into harmony with God. In the New Testament, the word for atonement is reconciliation. Reconciliation is the overall purpose for the grace of the Incarnation of Jesus. This is why the Incarnation of Jesus in history is the coming of a new reality in the history of humanity. The Scripture says, "Behold the Lamb of God, which taketh away the sin of the world [John 1:29]." Let it sink into your soul that there is, in the Incarnation of Jesus, an open door to the Father in heaven. This presents a far different spiritual truth than the perspective of an opened door to God in heaven. The Incarnation of Jesus presents the new divine possibility for us to become children of God. Jesus is the model for God's children. He shows us how to participate in the Father's power.

God's Power Flows Through Creation

The flow of God's power connects us to God through Jesus. The image of flowing is the best way to describe God's power in the coming of Jesus. God's power flows through everything in the same way a river flows through a land. Just as the Mississippi River brings vital life to the land through which it flows, God's power brings life to everything in its historical path. The flow of God's power is always historical. Consider the New Birth as a historical reality in the Incarnation of Jesus. The New Birth is the historical possibility of making new people in the world. Creation becomes the river through which God's power flows. It flows through everything that God creates. Creation itself is flowing. Creation responds to the original Mind of God. The Mind of God is the only original mind in Creation. God as original mind still keeps Creation on the path of God's intended purpose. Humanity is also on the created path of God's purpose because humanity is also part of the Creation. The only exception with humanity consists in its God given free will. However, God never alters his original purpose for any reason. The possibility for new people through Jesus Christ in the world always comes with the flow of God's power. This possibility existed even before the writing of the Old Testament. God has always possessed this power.

Possession, according to law, is ownership. God's possession of His flowing power, because it is still in his possession, attests to His ownership. Therefore it follows that, God still owns the Creation because it is still in His possession. God has not turned Creation over to humanity. God gives new life to the human race because it is still in His hands. Purpose is the defining principle of God's actions. It is the purpose of God to bring the Creation to the goals that He had in mind at the time of Creation. The Power of God in the physical world exists in the form of energy. In fact, in Creation, energy undergoes different forms. Jesus becomes our model for teaching us how to use God's energy.

You Can Study War No More

Our African American ancestors who sang *Give Me Jesus*, saw in Jesus the best human model for living. They lived in a constant state of survival warfare. Survival warfare characterizes their lives on this planet. War results from human greed. The scripture says, "From whence come wars and fighting among you? Come they not hence, even of the lusts that war in your members [James 4:1]"? Until our own Incarnation in Jesus Christ, we war within our self. This inner warfare puts us at war with Creation. Therefore, learning how to fight this war presents the human problem. We struggle with forces that we do not understand. However, we can learn from Jesus how to deal with these forces. Jesus taught us that for every force of evil there is an opposite equal force of good. The Scripture tells us to, "Overcome evil with good [Romans 12:21]." The law of physics also operates, as the law of Spirit, what is above is the same as below. The image of Jesus as the Lamb of God puts this picture of struggle in the right perspective. The Lamb of God slain from the foundation of the world presents a practical truth. The fact that Jesus was born to die for the new Creation reveals the divine truth that sin is already judged by God. Sinless, a state of perfection in the eyes of God, declares a state that no human being can meet. Therefore, the sinless Lamb of God came through the human birth channel, to meet the requirement of being without sin Himself, in order to die for our sins. As God's child, you can live without inner conflict because Jesus died. This reveals the meaning of the Incarnation of Jesus; the truth that the Lamb of God was slain from the foundation of the world for sinners.

It is useful to think of the word *conformation* as the act of development.

"Con" means with and "formation" means to form. Thus, conformation means "with formation." The resurrection following the death of Jesus is the essential part of the Incarnation of Jesus and presents your inner self "with formation" of New Birth. Resurrection means "with formation" of the Incarnation of Jesus as the Lamb of God for continuation of Creation. It consolidates the promise of connecting God and Creation. This truth was first expressed in these words, "And I will put enmity between you and the woman; He shall bruise you on the head, and you shall bruise him on the heel [Genesis 3:15]." The Incarnation of Jesus through the resurrection provides the blessing of this promise of renewal. The resurrection, therefore, is your validating blessing of renewal of Creation. God's validation is your only guarantee that can make an act acceptable to God. God can only validate that which is according to His will. God's integrity makes God obligated to be true to Himself. Jesus makes this renewal of Creation possible by His death on the cross. The word *justification* describes how God legally saves Creation. Justification satisfies the legal obligation of God to judge and forgive sin. God's moral integrity requires that He act consistently and justly. When God raised Jesus from the dead, justification as a legal means for salvation became possible. It is then and only then, that God blesses the Creation with new possibilities for divinity. Athanasius, one of the Early Church fathers, whose work about the Incarnation remains even today as one of the definitive statements of the three in one, God the Father, God the Son, and God the Holy Spirit, the doctrine of the one God in three persons, tells us that, "Jesus became human in order that we might become divine." Your inner conflict ends when Jesus becomes your role model. Once this happens then you can live in peace with yourself and with your fellowman.

Trust is More Than Belief

Trust in Jesus releases you from the fear of death. We learn from Jesus that trust is the main factor in the faith. Jesus absolutely depended upon God as a lifestyle of faith. His dependence on God is evidence of a genuine trust base. Jesus did everything with the trust that God would work out the details. Your unity with the Trinity requires that your faith in Jesus manifest your partnership with God. Your faith in Jesus is a trust rooted in Jesus' own dependence on His Father. Therefore, this faith unifies you and the Father. This unity held the bond together through all the suffering and sorrow of your life. Just as Jesus knew that He and the Father were one in purpose and in nature, you also can make the same claim. You can learn this model of trust when you realize that Jesus is your reminder of what it means to be God's child. The Incarnation of Jesus is the beginning of your unifying connection to the Father.

The idea of connection is the most significant idea in Incarnation Centered Spirituality. Connection means that there is continuity between two actions. Continuity is the sense that the ascension of Jesus means that the Father, the Son, the Holy Spirit, and the believers connects to the Incarnation of Jesus. Your initiation into the life of the Father continues in the ascension of Jesus. Jesus' going to the Father permits the coming of the Spirit from the Father as the continuation of Incarnation. In fact, the ascension of Jesus is part of your new life in Jesus. Fullness in Christ means that the ascension of Jesus is a complete part of the Saving Grace of God. Jesus models this Saving Grace for you to embrace as your own connection with the Father.

Conflict is Not Always a Bad Thing

Jesus overcame conflict by faith in the Father. Conflict means absence of peace. Conflict, however, is not the real problem that gives you the most trouble. Conflict also means an opportunity for growth. Conflict is the opportunity for learning a new way to confront life. Sometimes Jesus brings conflict into your life in order to give you peace. Jesus says, "Do not think that I came to bring peace on the earth; I did not come to bring peace, but a sword [Matthew 10: 34]." Reconciliation is the peace Jesus gives to those who are in an adversarial relationship with God. Even though reconciliation makes peace, some conflict comes with it. The peace that Jesus gives could never be possible with just his birth alone. Incarnation Centered Spirituality begins with the fact of Jesus' birth, because of the purpose of his death on the cross and its completion in his resurrection and his ascension. Jesus models how we should live with conflict. Incarnation Centered Spirituality is the lifestyle that lets you live with conflict. Embracing Jesus is the beginning of peace in your life. However, this is peace with conflict. Your embrace puts you in the body of Christ as well as it puts Christ in you. You must keep in your heart, head and hands that there is no possibility of the peace of Jesus without your New Birth in his Incarnation. Everything in your spiritual life starts with the Incarnation of Christ. Moreover, your New Birth begins with trusting in God's method of salvation. This method is your way of peace in conflict. This is what the cross symbolizes. The Scriptures says, "I have been crucified with Christ; and it is no longer I who live, but Christ lives in me; and the life which I now live in the flesh I live by faith in the Son of God, who loved me, and delivered himself up for me [Galatians 2:20]."

Real Liberation is in the Birth of Jesus

The highest goal of African Americans is liberation. Therefore, you must embrace, with all of your trust, the birth of Jesus. The birth of Jesus means the beginning of liberation in Jesus is available as Creation for all who put their trust in Jesus. Now that liberation in Jesus is available in Creation, communion with God is possible. Without Jesus in the history of humanity, there could be no communion with the Creator. This explains why nature suffers because of the destructive acts of man. Humanity has not seen that the liberating power of Jesus includes the Creation. Thus, the birth of Jesus has not entered into the consciousness of those who abuse the environment. Praise is the evidence that the liberation of Jesus is both as Creation and in Creation. When the birth of Jesus becomes part of your consciousness then the liberation of Jesus becomes available for you as part of Creation. The birth of Jesus continues your process of creation. This means that redemption continues your part of the Creation. Redemption means both liberation and community. The birth of Jesus, therefore, is the beginning of liberation and the death and resurrection of Jesus is the completion of your liberation. Redemption also means freedom from oppression. You must start thinking liberation. It is essential that you think and believe in your liberation in Jesus Christ. Remember you cannot become whole, until liberation from the forces that keep you bound to fear and failure becomes your conscious way of thinking.

Let your mind grasp the idea that Jesus is part of the Trinity. Pre-existence is the concept that says Jesus existed as the Son of God before Creation. This powerful concept makes it possible for humanity to make connection with the same divine Trinity that existed before the Creation. You must let the embrace of the Incarnation grasp the Trinity. The Trinity is the ultimate source of your liberation. The Godhead, which is the Trinity, exists and operates as the Father, the Son, and the Holy Spirit flowing throughout Creation in different modes and with different functions, but always flows in perfect harmony. Moreover, you must view this flowing as the intention of the Trinity. Intention, in this case, works to establish identity. It is the intention of the Trinity that causes the initiative acts of liberation throughout the Creation. In other words, liberation is flowing throughout the Creation. You must embrace this divine intention. This is why the intercessory prayer of Jesus is necessary. It was his role in the beginning to operate, as the agent of human liberation, as a human being, and yet remain part of the Trinity. You must understand the biblical difference between the Son of God and the Son of Man. Jesus made the choice to come into this world as the Son of Man to liberate all of humanity by being the reminder of what being God's child exemplifies.

Jesus is always Available to You

You can actually think just like Jesus. Jesus made a conscious decision to make his mind available to you. Choice is what makes the Mind of Jesus available to all of us today. It was Jesus' choice to come to earth as a human being. This choice made the Son of God the new humanity--the Son of Man. His mind is now available to all human beings through choice. Your choice is still essential in allowing the Mind of Jesus become part of your being. Your obedience is essential for the Mind of Jesus to operate through you. Jesus was obedient to the Father. His obedience is the reason why the Mind of Jesus is available to all of humanity today. Consequently, the obedience of Jesus is still necessary. It is clear that you must express the obedience of Jesus in your life, if you are to take advantage of the availability of the Mind of Jesus. You must be responsive to the call of God in Christ on your life just as Jesus was. Moreover, your responsiveness to the call of God is always the same requirement, just as it was before the creation of the universe, to yield to the Word of God. Before the Creation, the Trinity always chose to respond to each other. It is the choice of your head, the obedience of your heart, and the responsiveness of your hands that ultimately make the Mind of Jesus available for you now. Your ability to transcend the circumstances of life is in the healing power of Jesus through your choice.

You Must Rise Above Your Troubles

Just as the factual saying goes, "your troubles can get you down," the saying, "you must sink or swim" is also factual. It is clear that you must transcend your troubles. When you transcend your circumstances, you rise above your circumstances. In Jesus, we can live the life of transcendence. Transcendence works in conjunction with the healing of Jesus. It is what helps us to become new creatures in the head, heart, and hand. The healing power is in the vitality of the blood of Jesus. The blood of Jesus would be no good without the ability to help us transcend our circumstances in life. Vitality always comes with the real healing of Jesus in the Incarnation. The Incarnation of Jesus makes the possibility of raising above life's pitfalls a reality. The healing of Jesus is the transforming of dead life into living life. Living life performs works of life on both the physical and spiritual plane of humanity.

Allow your mind to gain a full understanding of the discipleship of Jesus. Disciples are followers who always walk in the path of their teacher. In fact, the true disciple is a true follower. The true disciple imitates the teacher. As you seek knowledge from Jesus, you are always the disciple. Knowledge changes things. Change is what seekers are looking for, when they take a path, the leader is walking. This is why the true disciple of Jesus is also able to do as the Master. To become a healer is the greatest aspiration a disciple of Jesus desires. The genuine disciple of Jesus is the sincere representative of Jesus Christ as a healer in the world today. Healers are first able to overcome their circumstances.

Your healing behavior must be able to overcome your own troubling circumstances. Your behavior should represent Jesus. When the world sees your behavior, it should be able to see Jesus. Behavior of believers is the only image of Jesus seen by others. Behavior is the only thing evaluated in the person who claims to be a disciple of Jesus because the only authentic behavior is rooted in truth that reflects divinity in the world. The core of life is the innermost part of the believer that reflects the personality of Jesus. No one can see your core, until you engage in some kind of behavior. Hence, others only feel but can never see the Spirit. The personality of Jesus, in the believer, is the action that represents Jesus Christ in the circumstances of life, which can be seen. This is crucial to keep in mind.

Believe in Miracles

Miracles operate according to natural laws. Therefore, the argument that a miracle must operate outside of natural law is not absolute truth. The provisions of Jesus come through natural law. In fact, the provision of Jesus must come through natural law. Manners are as important as means. The means by which things are done is as important as the manner in which they are done. Manners and means are not quite the same thing. Manners come from the heart while means come from the head. The reason God loves a cheerful giver is because the receiver can discern the giver's feelings. The provisions of Jesus always come from a cheerful giver. The cheerful giver is under the influence of Sanctifying Grace. In Chapter 4, you will learn more about the tool of Sanctifying Grace.

Chapter 4

The Power of Sanctifying Grace

Lord, I want to be a Christian in-a my heart,
Lord, I want to be a Christian in-a my heart.
Lord, I want to be a Christian in-a my heart.
I don't want to be like Judas in-a my heart.
In-a my heart. I don't want to be like Judas
In-a my heart.

The Negro spiritual, "Lord I Want to Be a Christian" declares that Sanctifying Grace is a matter of the interior life. The Path of the Via Positiva is the pathway of Sanctifying Grace in the journey to wholeness. Interior life is the very depth of the soul. The interior life is lived deeply in the soul; it is the life of your whole person, ...your intellectual life, your scientific, creative or homeboy life. Therefore, your interior life is essentially your knowledge of God, love of God and your love of man for God's sake. Nevertheless, as natural man, you do not know God, love God, nor love man for God's sake. Therefore, your conversion experience equipped you with Sanctifying Grace to meet the spiritual demands. However, even after conversion, many Christians are not capable of knowing God, loving God, or loving man for God's sake. Unfortunately, many Christians have accepted the teaching that faith in Christ guarantees salvation as once saved always saved which still leaves them with a shallow spiritual life. They neglect Sanctifying Grace, the other important teaching of the spiritual life. Your African Americans ancestors who produced the above spirituals knew that Sanctifying Grace is the only way they could be Christians in their hearts. Thus, they prayed, "Lord I want to be a Christian in my heart."

Sanctifying Grace is the principle of the interior life. It is the tool of Embracing the Incarnation. It makes us truly children of God because it lets us partake of God's divine nature, the supernatural life that is love, good works, and the ability to get beyond self and to truly love truth and goodness, more than self. Sanctification is, in fact, the act of God's grace making us partakers of God's divine nature as the growth in Incarnation. You must embrace Sanctifying Grace as a gift from God. Essentially, Sanctifying Grace gives you the ability to live the life of divinity on earth. This ability characterizes Sanctifying Grace. Sanctifying Grace, more specifically, gives you ability to live Incarnation Centered Spirituality. Embracing the tool of Sanctifying Grace is the tool of the Via Positiva. More importantly, this tool of Sanctifying Grace is the tool of Incarnation. When you embrace the Incarnation of Jesus, you convert to a supernatural life in Christ. This supernatural life has the ability to grow toward wholeness. This ability to grow toward wholeness, significantly, is the greatest divine power that comes with Sanctifying Grace. It comes as the direction of faith in the Incarnation of Jesus. The direction of this faith is automatically in Sanctifying Grace. Therefore, the direction of Incarnation Center Spirituality is rooted in Sanctifying Grace. If there were no direction toward wholeness in Incarnation Centered Spirituality, then there would be no profit in living this five-fold path. The five-fold path to wholeness is the lifestyle of living in Incarnation Centered Spirituality. The spiritual progress could not move in the direction of wholeness, unless the seed of wholeness already existed in you, a seed of the same nature as the wholeness toward, which you are moving.

Love is the power that gives Sanctifying Grace the sphere within which to operate. Moreover, Sanctifying Grace makes love possible. You must see love as the fertile soil in which all healing is located. When you think about Sanctifying Grace, you are also thinking about love. Sanctifying Grace is the love of God working in your life to make you whole. Sanctifying Grace also ignites the image of God in your center.

The Image of God is the ultimate objective of Sanctifying Grace. The Image of God is the seed that the spiritual fathers recognized in the innermost part of the soul as the same Image God meant in the creation of man. The Spirit of God ignites this Image when He brings life to the original Creation in your interior life. Sanctifying Grace operates on the seed of eternal life to give wholeness of life to the saved person. The intention of God makes itself known through this seed of eternal life. God has a plan, which has been His intention from the foundation of the world. His intention was and is to bring creation into His divine purpose according to His eternal will. Sanctifying Grace helps us to operate within the intentions of God. Everything has within it the intention of God. Human beings are not the only creations that possess the intention of God. The eternal presence of God possesses God's intentions. God's presence never leaves Creation. This is not to suggest that God is in everything. God is always outside of Creation. The presence of God is not the person of God. When you stop and think about it, you realize that presence is an undeniable reality in Creation. Presence makes all the difference in the world. Everything has presence. The presence of eternal life as the Image of God, lying dormant in the interior of humanity, makes Sanctifying Grace necessary. If there were no presence of eternal life, there would be no possibility of Sanctifying Grace. Sanctifying Grace comes with faith in Christ. Sanctifying Grace, not faith alone, empowers the believer to walk the path of the Holy Spirit, which is strict spiritual discipline. Unfortunately, it is becoming increasingly clear that many believers in the African American segment of the Church today think salvation requires no spiritual discipline. Essentially, Sanctifying Grace gives you the desire for spiritual discipline. When you embraced the Incarnation of Jesus, you received your Sanctifying Grace as the beginning of the spiritual discipline you needed to travel the five-fold path to wholeness. Baptism is the symbol of Sanctifying Grace.

The Spirit of God makes baptism the image of Sanctifying Grace for believers. Baptism is the outward sign that a supernatural change has happened in the interior life of the believer. The presence of Sanctifying Grace is in baptism. Moreover, this is also evidence that Sanctifying Grace is making its power felt in the believer's life. Salvation is not something that you feel emotionally. Salvation deals with the sin problem. Salvation positively blots out your sins by the infusion of the new life of grace and love. This spiritual endowment is evidence that there is a spiritual power at work in your interior self. This power defines your personhood. The understanding of personhood becomes very important at this point. Person as a whole personality becomes the norm. You receive the empowerment for complete expression of the divine presence that is in your personality. You, in fact, become an Incarnate Word of God. After all, Jesus, the Word of God, first became flesh in order that you might become an Incarnate Word. The empowerment of Sanctifying Grace in your baptism permits you to symbolically die and to be resurrected with Jesus. This outward baptism is a sign that there is an inward baptism of the Holy Spirit completing your inner conversion. This explanation shows that baptism becomes the means of Sanctifying Grace for believers. It is more than just a symbol of conversion. It is the evidence of Sanctifying Grace revealing God's plan. God's plan always exists before the manifestation. God plans everything to the final degree, before he reveals it. When God says "Let there be," He has already seen the total picture. God is God because God does not have to see things in a passing parade. He sees at once, the entire parade from start to finish. God sees His Image in your interior life. God put it there! God has original plans for your interior self. God never deviates from His original plan. To this extent, it is essential to understand that interior life is your true self.

Originality is Still in the Interior Life

Remember only God is original. Sanctifying Grace permits us to participate in God's originality. We must resist the need to recreate ourselves. God has the blueprint. Only originality is said of God. Nothing else is original, therefore, everything else is simply a copy of that which already exists in the Mind of God. We cannot create anything. We can only reproduce things. Art is the reproduction of that which already exists. In our false self, it is easy to forget that originality is only of God. Our thoughts let us express what is in our minds, but our thoughts are not original. There is nothing new under the sun. Our thoughts are shaped by what we are conditioned to think. Sanctifying Grace is most necessary to help us remember the originality of God. It is easy for us to forget we are products of culture. Culture plays a great part in our understanding of reality. Our worldview is primarily the expression of our experiences of culture in which we are developed.

Sanctifying Grace teaches us to participate in originality instead of trying to be original. Sanctifying Grace helps you to trust the fact that originality is in the interior self. Therefore, you have an interior self because Sanctifying Grace must have an original substance upon which to work. The interior self is the only part of humanity that God maintained in the fall of Adam. This means that the only thing Sanctifying Grace can use in the believer's life is the Image of God. Sanctifying Grace empowers the heart to express passion. This passion makes the love of God active in the life of the believer. Because of this passion, the believer is able to know and love God, and to love man for God's sake. Our hearts experience Sanctifying Grace on the level of pathos. Pathos fuels us with the emotions needed to initiate actions of compassion in the world. Compassion is of God. Only the Word of God produces compassion in the hearts of believers. This is what Jesus means when He says, "Should not thou also have had compassion on thy fellow servant even as I had pity on thee [Matthew 18:33]?"

The ultimate empowerment of Sanctifying Grace is our ability to know and to love only God and man for God's sake. Sanctifying Grace is an extension of heaven on earth. The full and complete development of the interior life is wholeness, which is eternal life expressed in the world. The Holy Spirit is the presence of this extension of heaven on earth. The Holy Spirit's presence is the promise Jesus made to His disciples before He returned to heaven. This promise makes the extension of heaven a reality in the lives of the believers. When Jesus was in earth, in Him heaven was also present in earth. This path of embracing the Incarnation of the Son of God is the open reception of truth in our interior self. We openly acknowledged that the Kingdom of God is already here in the world. Sanctifying Grace enables us to operate in the Kingdom of God. The presence of the Holy Spirit makes the Kingdom of God function in the world according to the plan of God. The Holy Trinity is now a reality on earth as the Kingdom of God. The practical presence of the Trinity is the complete presence of the Godhead in our interior self. You use the presence of Sanctifying Grace to participate in the Trinity. The Holy Spirit fulfills the promise of Jesus. He produces the fruit of Sanctifying Grace. Fruit is a common word Jesus used to identify the authenticity of believers. This is the promise of Sanctifying Grace for growing into the image and likeness of Jesus Christ, which is ultimate authenticity. The fruit of the Holy Spirit is proof positive that a supernatural power is working in the life of believers. Sanctifying Grace depends ultimately on how the believer makes use of the growth possibility in the interior life, through spiritual discipline. Sanctifying Grace is more that a touch of divinity. It is divinity.

You Can Become Complete in This Life

The ultimate experience of Incarnation Centered Spirituality is wholeness. Wholeness is completion. Completion is an important element that you should understand in order to understand Sanctifying Grace. We might consider other things about the value of Sanctifying Grace in the life of believers, but completeness is the ultimate experience. Completion is paramount. You embraced the conviction of wholeness when you embraced Incarnation. Conviction should be highly valued in the life of the believer. In fact, conviction is the primary act of Sanctifying Grace. If there is no conviction, then there is no salvation in the first place. Likewise, if there is no conviction after salvation, there is no growth.

Sanctifying Grace produces contemplation that is rooted in the conviction that Jesus is the Incarnate Son of God. Contemplation is a prayer life that helps the believer walk in the Spirit. The tool of Sanctifying Grace in Incarnation Centered Spirituality is in the Spirit. In the embracing of Incarnation we encounter three important values of Sanctifying Grace. The three values of Sanctifying Grace are completion, conviction, and contemplation. They are the gifts of Sanctifying Grace, without which there is no spiritual means of walking the five-fold path of Incarnation Centered Spirituality. Sanctifying Grace also operates through nature. Sanctifying Grace makes natural things become supernatural. That which is supernatural was once natural. Nature defines the essence of a thing. However, it really is more than this; it is the primary identifying part of what a thing is in its essence. Nevertheless, nature in reality changes in essence. Sanctifying Grace, however, remains unchanged in nature. Sanctifying Grace is the continuous unchanging presence of divinity in the life of the believer. Responding to God is the natural thing to do when Sanctifying Grace is present in a believer's life. The believer hears a voice deep within the inner life; the inner self, the true self and interior life are the same, and answers with a total response. The shape of this response is always in the form of contemplative prayer. These examples show how Sanctifying Grace is a force for spiritual change in the life of the believer. When there is no Sanctifying Grace, there is no divinity in the life of the person. You should expect divinity in your life after your conversion. Divinity grows as it moves towards wholeness. You develop divine expectations in life as you grow spiritually.

Expectation Makes it Happen

Expectation is why anything in your life increases. Increase works according to the law of divine purpose. Capacity regulates increase. Nothing can grow beyond its capacity. Capacity in this case is expectation. Capacity is the limitation of increase. Growth works according to the law of growth. Spiritual power can be seen. Therefore, it can be measured. The spiritual law of growth is the same as the natural law of growth. There is only one law. Your expectations become energy for growth in your life. Spiritual energy is the ability to make it known. Energy acts upon substance.

Substance is the faith of expectation. If there is no substance of faith, there is no spiritual growth. Emotions play an important role in spiritual growth. The positive and most powerful emotion is love. Love is the real motive behind will. Emotion is always the fixed boundaries of the believer's lifestyle in the world. You can increase your boundaries by adjusting your emotions. Your emotions will always influence your actions. Your deep sense of responsibility determines the emotions that direct your actions. Your welfare is always riding on your emotions. Sanctifying Grace always requires emotional balance for believers in every situation. Sanctifying Grace will regulate the emotions in your life if you will let it. Your sin will always prevent its regulating power.

Fallen Nature is a Fact

Sanctifying Grace helps us to move beyond the fallen nature of duality. Fallen nature is a concept of Christian thinking about the nature of humanity. Some call it *original sin*. Nevertheless, it is because of the fallen condition that language has lost the ability to guide humanity. Moreover, language is also in a fallen state. Language is also shaped by culture. Therefore, you need to be aware that culture produces language. Our system of communication and beliefs are products of our language. This is how powerful people control society. Sanctifying Grace protects you from those who have power to control language. Sanctifying Grace produces wisdom to know that those who control the discourse are always those who control society. The discourse is the limitation of the thought process. The status quo remains the same until some brave soul takes a stand and asks why. This is why the understanding of language must be controlled by Sanctifying Grace. Nothing, of importance in your life will happen, until your understanding of language is purified.

The desert is the place where early spiritual masters went to purify their language. They would take the journey into the desert to get control of their spiritual lives in the world. This is how they understand their calling. They knew this is necessary to live their purpose of changing the world. After they lived there for the time necessary to cleanse their souls and have a real commitment to grow in the Spirit and likeness of Jesus Christ, they would come out for their work.

Creative living always required the desert experience. There could be no power to create the life that would bring the kind of change in the world that makes the spiritual life possible. You must identify with the spiritual masters of old. They showed the way to spiritual wholeness. Identification is most important to the spiritual life because it is personal. If you do not know who you are according to God's purpose, then you can never know God's purpose for you in your life. You need your identity to embrace Sanctifying Grace. You must take time to consider what Sanctifying Grace really means in your life. Until you fully understand what Sanctifying Grace means in your lifetime your ability to journey the five-fold path of Incarnation Centered Spirituality is limited.

You See God through your Pure Heart

Single mindedness is the pure heart of the sanctified believer. A pure heart is always within the grasp of the believer who would become single-minded. Single-mindedness is the one thought that controls the behavior of the believer under all circumstances. It is the ability to will one thing. This means that which is all around us. We just have to be aware that at all times we are to have one mind. Intention is, as we have said, the only way God works. Intention is always the Mind of God at work. Intention is single-mindedness. When you embrace the intention of God, then you embrace the new single-mindedness of the believer. This is the only means of Sanctifying Grace operating in the believer. Moreover, the believer's intention must be the same as God's in order to have single-mindedness. It is only through our purpose that we express our thinking. Therefore, our purpose is the medium in which single-mindedness is revealed. Single-mindedness is not something that we can achieve of our own will. It has to be produced by the pure heart of Sanctifying Grace. Sanctifying Grace is the means of our obtaining the pureness of heart. Faith is the only way we receive a pure heart.

Faith is the means by which we embrace infinity. Infinity is also the ultimate reality about which many spiritual masters speak. What we seek in the spiritual journey is union with the ultimate reality. Faith works the good works of God. Moreover, only in infinity, does the good works of God take place. This is why a pure heart is necessary. We cannot produce good works without a pure heart. When good works takes place in the world it is because of Sanctifying Grace.

Hope is the expectation of infinity. Infinity is like air. It is already all around us. We don't realize that air is around us until we cannot breath. Then we know that air is a real part of our existence in the world. So is infinity. Faith makes it possible for us to seek infinity. Hope is the expectation that infinity can be. When we become convinced that faith has made it possible to embrace infinity then infinity becomes something we expect to realize and we start out to accomplish it. Love is what keeps us going. It is because the love of God is in our hearts that we are compelled to embrace infinity. The sanctified believer has in his true self, the power of faith, hope, and love that keeps seeking to embrace infinity in all situations in life. By true self, I mean the interior life. Seeking to embrace, to experience a personal encounter with infinity is the journey of Incarnation Centered Spirituality. Now we have seen what positive assertions about the Creator are possible; in Part II, of the E.A.G.L.E. Technique, you will discover the method for refocusing your affection. In Chapter 5 through Chapter 8, you will read about controlling your affections. This is the Path of the Via Negativa.

PATH II

THE VIA NEGATIVA
CONTROLLING YOUR AFFECTIONS

Chapter 5

Engaging in the Riverside Experience

Going to put on my long white robe,
Down by the riverside, down by
the riverside, down by the riverside.
I ain't going to study war no more, ain't
Going to study to war no more, ain't
Going to study war no more.
Going to put on my golden shoes, down
By the riverside, down by the riverside.

Chapter 5 is about the riverside experience. The riverside experience is what enslaved African Americans, in the early history of this country, discovered for soul survival. This riverside experience is what historians refer to as the "Invisible Institution." The Invisible Institution is the beginning of the Black Church, Black Religion, in this country. The riverside experience is the path slaves used to purify their affections in order to find freedom and identification in their understanding of God. They discovered that they could have neither in the slave master's concept of God. Therefore, if you are serious about Incarnation Centered Spirituality, you will also have to travel through the wilderness to go down by the riverside. This journey is inward. Today this same Black Religion serves as the source for contemporary development of Black Spirituality and Black Theology. What is now Black Theology was first Black Spirituality for survival of the soul. Black Spirituality, now as then, starts with embracing the Incarnation. You embraced the Incarnation of Jesus Christ in Part I. Now, in Part II you will start the journey on the pathway of purifying your affections. You start this journey of purification for the same reasons early African Americans started their journey. You must purify the affections. Indeed, you must also be able to recognize your affections. Most of us confuse our intellect with our affect. There is also the danger that you might love the plantation mentality. You might be confused about your thinking and your feelings. You think you are thinking about something, when in fact, you are feeling about something, and trying to reach a valid conclusion through your affection or emotion.

You Must Go into the Wilderness

The wilderness is the solitary trip to the riverside. Significantly, the purifying experience begins with the trip into the wilderness. Thus, it is in the wilderness where your focus on purification is established and maintained. Focus is an important part of purification. Purification, above everything else on this spiritual journey, is the purpose for the riverside experience. The focus down by the riverside is still on freedom, justice, and identity. Likewise, this is the same focus of Incarnation Centered Spirituality. Moreover, the tool of the riverside is your tool of purification from all things, including all ideas and all emotions that keep you from wholeness. Freedom, justice, and identity, the ultimate purposes in the riverside struggle of the Early Black Church, remain the primary goals today. Personal wholeness demands both freedom and identity. Your own self-imposed slavery to things, ideas, and emotions keep you chained to your false self. Your false self is your broken self. Therefore, you need to work for the liberation of your true self by letting go of the negative affections that keep you chained to your false self. You must develop the single-mindedness that concentrates only on the God beyond God who is the ultimate object of our positive affections. The best way to describe this principle of single-mindedness is that it is the act of letting go and letting be. You focus only on the God beyond God who sets you free from duplicity and keeps you on the path of self-discipline. Self-discipline is your control of your emotions. Self-discipline is learning to let the Holy Spirit control your life instead of your false-self controlling your life.

Therefore, self-discipline is essential. Self-discipline is equally essential for the journey of purification. You have to let go and let be. The decision to let go and let be is the act of entering into the Path of the Via Negativa, about which the early spiritual masters spoke. This is the negative way where self-discipline is developed. In the Via Negativa, we enter the darkness where we confront the hidden things in our soul, and in our society. In this pathway, we face the pain of our own bitterness and doubts in the darkness of our soul. Here we enter into the innermost part of our being, our interior self. You can call this the pathway or whatever you want to call it. However, just remember you must enter into the darkness of your interior self, if you are to journey along the pathway of purifying your affections. Purification is the unifying purpose for entering the darkness. Our affirmation in Part I of the Turner E.A.G.L.E. Technique, the Path of Via Positiva, is the positive embracing of the Incarnate Son of God. The immediate result is your dissatisfaction with the world systems, the plantations. Dissatisfaction originates in the embrace of the Incarnation. If there is no dissatisfaction in your soul, then you will not enter into the darkness of the Via Negativa. Moreover, dissatisfaction is part of the spiritual struggle that results in the riverside experience. If there were no dissatisfaction with the world systems in your life, you would never confront the things you need to change in life. God has created the soul such that it cannot tolerate dissatisfaction. The interior self will not tolerate imperfection, which is the cause of our dissatisfaction. Deep in our inner self, there is the ultimate perfection of Creation, the Image of God. This is the very reason that there is a personal riverside journey to wholeness. By our dissatisfaction, God calls us into the darkness. The soul seeks wholeness.

The soul knows what it needs in order to find wholeness. The soul needs a religion to address its brokenness. It does not matter what the religion is, as evidenced by the many different kinds of spirituality in the world today. The soul uses religion to seek the satisfaction of wholeness. Moreover, this happens even if the soul has to invent a religion to produce the necessary elements to develop a belief system for wholeness. We already have such a religion in Jesus Christ. Jesus helped us to understand the pathway to nothingness. The Path of the Via Negativa is the pathway that leads to the discovery of our nothingness. Therefore, the pathway of our nothingness creates a great sense of Lostness in our lives. We do really want to keep our affections as they are, even though we let them go. Thus, the Path of the Via Negativa is the pathway of grief. We grieve over our Lostness in the darkness of the Path of the Via Negativa. Lostness is a very powerful feeling. We feel the emptiness created by the sense of nothingness. Moreover, the emptiness causes our souls to seek the fulfillment. Therefore, we should never try to cover up the grief, nor deny the emptiness, this, after all, is why we enter the pathway of the Via Negativa where everything in our soul is uncovered. We must remain open to the nothingness of our interior darkness. The early African Americans in slavery, experiencing the feeling of having lost the essentials of their humanity, made the riverside journey into the wilderness seeking their wholeness. They looked for closure by passing through the darkness. Closure is important in the grieving process. As we learned from the early African Americans, the soul is seeking wholeness through closure. Therefore, this seeking for a resolution from the sense of Lostness is not a one-time thing; it is a series of purifying experiences along the pathway of the Via Negativa. In other words, the purifying experiences continue until there is a replacement of negative affections with positive affections.

Positive affection is divine "love for God and man for God's sakes."[8] Positive affection is the commandment of God. We read of the positive affections in Deuteronomy 6:4-6, as Moses says, "Hear, O Israel! The Lord is our God, the Lord is one! And you shall Love the Lord your God with all your heart and with all your soul and with all your might." Jesus later reaffirms this commandment with a new emphasis. He taught his disciples this new emphasis in John 13:34, he says, "A new commandment I give to you, that you love one another, even as I have love, that you also love one another." You can see a new emphasis in this commandment. The new emphasis is, love one another "as Jesus has loved you." You embraced this same positive affection when you embraced the Incarnation in the Path of the Via Positiva in Part I of the Turner E.A.G.L.E. Technique. The possibility of positive affection makes us aware of the negative affection that keeps the enslaved chained to the plantation.

The significance of Part II of the Turner E.A.G.L.E. Technique is that you are able to recognize your negative affections. Negative affections such as hatred, greed, and other negative affections are learned. Those embracing Incarnation Centered Spirituality, seek to replace negative affections with the divine love of the Creator. Essentially, we are seeking a positive soul. The positive soul is the true self. Unfortunately, we have learned to live with the negative soul, the false self, for so long, until we have lost sight of the positive soul, the true self. Nevertheless, the positive soul has always been in the innermost center of our being. We will learn how to use the technique of Affection on the pathway to reconnect to our positive soul. Until you make the connection with your true self, you will feel empty. However, remember emptiness does not mean that there is a vacuum in the inner self; this is the true self.

In Spirituality Emptiness is Also Substance

Emptiness means that something is completely missing, but not everything. However, it does not necessarily mean that there is entirely nothing there. We commonly think of a totally void space when we think of emptiness; however, emptiness in spirituality is still substance. A good example of this is the fact that a cup of coffee can be empty of sugar and yet the cup is still full of coffee. In spirituality, the soul can be missing something and yet not be totally empty. When we think of emptiness in this way, we will understand what St. John of the Cross means by the dark night of the soul.[9] The soul must relearn to deprive itself of the desires for material things of this world. As you, deprive yourself of desires for material things of this world, your faith increases. As the faith, increases you go deeper into the inner self until you reconnect with your true self. You journey by faith until you understand that what you seek is wholeness in the God beyond God. By faith, you continue until you finally come to the God beyond God, who is substantially the darkness of divine mystery. On the pathway of the Via Negativa, you must, according to St. John of the Cross, pass through three dark nights, in order to come to unity with the God beyond God. "The three parts of the night are as a single night. The first part, which is about the senses, is the same as the beginning of the night in a single night. Things begin to fade from our sight and lose their form. The second part of the night, is as the darkest part of the single night; here we must walk by faith alone. The third part of the night is like the single night breaking into day. We begin to see better in the third part of the dark night,"[10] as stated earlier. The dark night of the soul is a single night with three parts. In the Turner E.A.G.L.E. Technique, the pathway of the dark night of the soul is a necessary riverside experience. When you become aware of the dark night, the riverside struggle truly becomes meaningful. Faith takes you through the darkness with a confidence unmatched by anything else. Faith makes the pathway of the Via Negativa a joyful, instead of an unhappy, experience. We sense the nothingness of the dark night and yet we feel fulfilled. God leads us into the dark night. God makes us aware that we must leave the dissatisfaction of our negative affections behind and enter into the darkness. When we recognize the dark night of the soul, as a necessary experience for wholeness, we let go and let be. We believe God is restoring positive affections in place of negative affections. As we enter into the darkness, we experience, instead of self-sufficiency, a profound dependency upon God. This leads to a sense of personal humility. Moreover, we sense that this humility is the mark of an authentic desire for wholeness. We become aware that the false self of negative affections prevents our humility. Our healing becomes apparent as our affections line up with God's will. Humility is God's will.

Humility is Letting God Be

Humility replaces our self-sufficiency of arrogance with our sensitivity to God at work in our inner self. We accept this truth even though we cannot scientifically prove it. Humility, after all, is the reason we enter the riverside experience. Humility must be rediscovered. Humility reveals the knowledge that God is in the center of our being. God placed this knowledge in our inner self at the beginning of Creation. Significantly, the rediscovery of this inner knowledge is an ongoing process of relearning what you have forgotten. The early spiritual masters called this knowledge "gnosis." Do not confuse gnosis with Gnosticism, the heresy rightly condemned by the Christian Church. The word gnosis is much earlier than Gnosticism. Gnosis means the interior or spiritual knowledge. Gnosis is knowledge of eternal truths revealed through interior illumination by the Spirit of God. This knowledge is unrecognized until we rediscover it, sometimes by chance, but more than likely, by a systematic strategy of relearning the innermost truths of the true self, through self-discipline. We still have divine wisdom in our true self; it survived the fall of Adam. This wisdom makes us humble. The problem for us is that we have learned to live in our false self. We need an encounter with the angels. Like Jacob, we need a new name. Recall the story of Jacob, in the Book of Genesis, wrestling with the angels. It is also necessary that you wrestle with angels down by the riverside, in the dark night of the soul. You should thank God for this angelic encounter and your arrival to your new reality. This encounter reveals the presence of an Ultimate Reality of the Creator. Ultimate Reality, in the truest sense, is always inside of us. We are carriers of this reality. Ultimate Reality is the wisdom of the inner self. The broken self responded to the affirmation and became restless. Therefore, the first place we want to go after embracing the Incarnation is down by the riverside where we can wrestle with the angels. After our false self comes face to face with our true self down by the riverside, our true self struggles to get out. At this point, it becomes your struggle to free the true self. This is our angelic struggle. Our negative affections become the baggage we need to let go. As we let go our affections, also known as our emotions, change.

The Affections Will Change

The change of affections starts as soon as you start the journey on the Path of the Via Negativa. This change of affections is also a sign that you are in a fight with the angels. The angels will leave you with a limp. You will walk forever with a slight limp. You will rediscover humility. You are not so sure now that you know everything as you did before the struggle. The sense of self-sufficiency leaves you. You sense that there is always more to life than what meets the eye. You have a change in taste. You see the beauty in Creation as you have never seen before. The inner eye, the eye of the true self, or the third eye, opens up to a new way of seeing. You start seeing from the inside out. You begin to understand that the mind is much more than the brain. You learned that mind is cosmic intelligence and that the mind is just one with the Creator. This Mind of the Creator is the cosmic mind in which we participate more so than a mind that we possess. This spiritual knowledge does not become clear to us until, we have wrestled with the angels down by the riverside. Fortunately, for us, the angels are in the riverside experience. When the angels defeat us, when spiritual knowledge changes our affections, and when our limp humbles us, then it becomes clear to us why wrestling with the angels is an important part of Incarnation Centered Spirituality and the five-fold path to wholeness.

Look for the Inner Conflict

On the pathway of Via Negativa, you must expect an inner conflict between that which is true and that, which is similar. We use the word true here instead of the word truth to be about things and people that are tested at every turn of the journey. The word true is used here in the sense of validation. The idea here is that a thing is true according to its purpose. Your perception is what is really being tested. The perception can be real and logical while at the same time it may not be true to its purpose. We often get logical confused with true. You need to be aware that in this sense true is only a measuring tool. When a thing is true, it is uniquely one of a kind. There cannot be two different kinds of the same thing and both be true in the sense of our word true. That which is true is not an imitation. If it is an imitation, then it may look like the original, but it is not the original. Only the original can be true. It must meet the requirement of "true blue." In this case, the search, for that which is true, is the search for that which is original. We have the true image of God in our inner being and the true spiritual knowledge. The perception must be original. Original perception is always that which sees what is already in the mix of things. Original perception is what God sees in the beginning. Understand that differentiation is always a secondary occurrence. It is that which lets us know that it is not the original. Now there is nothing wrong with differentiation. Differentiation is in fact how the cosmos keeps extending and enlarging into the forms that come into being and pass away. The cosmos is always churning away bringing into being new forms of being. This is because the cosmos is alive and its primary purpose is to give birth to new things. We can only perceive that which is essentially true, when we realize that differentiation is part of disciplined perception. Self-discipline operates within perception. In the perception is also the discipline of the self. Consistency in the discipline of our self operates within our perception. We can see only what we are ready to see. There is no way that we can perceive spiritual reality in the cosmos, until we have disciplined ourselves to receive, perceive, and conceive the reality, which characterizes that which is original. Spiritual reality is original. This is why testing new perceptions is an essential strategy we must develop down by the riverside, before trying to move down the five-fold path of wholeness. Positive affections make us free to act out our original role in life. We are ready to leave the riverside and travel the Via Negativa toward wholeness using the tool of Direction with the technique of Affection. At this point in the journey, directions become very important. The tool of direction is also the tool of affection purifications.

Chapter 6

Finding the Directions Before You Depart

Oh, my good Lord, show me de way.
Enter de chariot, travel along.
Noah sent out a mourn-in' dove,
Enter de chariot, travel along,
Which brought back a token of a heabn-ly love,
Gwinter serve my God while I have breath,
Enter de chariot, travel along.
So I can see Jesus after death.
Oh, My good Lord, show me de way.

"Oh, my good Lord, show me de way." This is the prayer of the African American traveling to freedom, justice and identity. The enslaved singers of this spiritual knew that they would need the help of God to travel to freedom, justice, and identity. This is the Path of the Via Negativa. The enslaved singers left the plantation and traveled through the wilderness to the riverside. On this Path of the Via Negativa, you are also leaving the riverside now to travel the rest of the path of the Via Negativa using the technique of affection with the tool of directions. It is time for you to travel deeper inwardly. Therefore, it is very necessary for you to know the direction in which you are traveling on your spiritual journey. You will need to ask to be shown the way. It is possible to develop serious psychological problems in the practice of spiritually. Thus, it is important to know if you are traveling to a serious problem or to a positive spiritual life. A breakthrough followed as we left the plantation and went into the wilderness. The breakthrough made us aware that God is calling us to freedom, justice, and identity.

The direction to the right path begins with the breakthrough. We cannot make the journey until we have the breakthrough. We must first come from behind negative affections blocking our path before we can be sure of our direction. As we have seen, the blockage in our path is our veil of affections. The fact of the matter is we really like the plantation. This is why we had to go down by the riverside. It is down by the riverside where we rethink what John says about loving the world. He says, "Do not love the world or things in the world. If anyone loves the world, the love of the Father is not in him [1John 2:15]." The riverside is where we discovered the right direction by detaching from negative emotions. Until the riverside, we might actually be going deeper into the plantation, rather than leaving. It takes courage to leave the little security the plantation offers. For our purpose, we may identify the world system as the plantation. In Western society, the world is the plantation for African and African American people. This is why we must deal with our veil of affections before we can be sure of our direction. It is hard to realize that we are stuck behind the veil of affections because the veil is so much a part of our false self. We actually think the veil of affections is normal.

Now, lifting the veil is not a normal process because it is more like cutting out our eyes. This explains why the technique of Affection began in the wilderness. You left the plantation and traveled through the wilderness to the riverside. You are now leaving the riverside. Therefore, you must be sure you have located the direction that leads toward your wholeness. Down by the riverside, you discovered and decided to let go of your affections that prevent you from having freedom and identity. Moreover, until we know this, we will never try to lift the veil. Affections are learned behavior. It must become apparent to us that we cannot lift the veil because we do not know that it is there. We discovered this when we left the plantation for the riverside. Incarnation Centered Spirituality leads us inward along the five-fold path to where we discover the need to know our direction. It is not until we begin Incarnation Centered Spirituality, that we gain the awareness, that we can raise the veil of affection.

You Must Turn to What You Need

As we travel inward from the riverside, we turn to what we need. Repentance is turning from negative affections to positive affirmations. Turning in life is a correction of direction. So, repentance is a necessity. Yet, turning in life is more than just changing our directions; it is also changing our person. We are tripartite beings having spirit, soul, and body. The body is the material part of our being; the soul is the animal part of our being, and the spirit is the function of our rational life. When the self or what we call the soul, is still pointing in a certain direction, then the other parts of our being must go in that direction or become separated. However, all parts can be in the same direction but still not be in agreement with each other. This is why we are broken people until we can pull ourselves together in agreement. The body can go in one direction, while the soul is going in another direction, and the spirit is going in a totally different direction. Moreover, the worst thing is that neither part knows the direction that the other parts are taking. Therefore, it is absolutely, necessary that repentance is part of the directions. Sorrow and pain can bring us to a point where we realize that we are going in the wrong direction. Then, each part cries out for the other parts. Hence, until our parts are unified, we are shattered and broken. We must turn from negative affections to positive affections. This is what the Scriptures teach. In 1 John 2:15, we are told, "Do not love the world, nor the things in the world. If any one loves the world, the love of the Father is not in him."

Remember, we are still in the dark night of the soul. In fact, this is the darkest part of the dark night. It is a cloud of unknowingness. We can only trust that God is leading us through the dark night. We can only obey! We only know that we can accept our self, and our God as the ground of our be- ing. Our determination is to reach out to the God beyond God and to love God, who is beyond our ability to know, He enables us to know that He first loved us. However, we learn that we do not know how to obey. We know that if we keep going in the wrong direction, we will go further away from our other parts. Furthermore, in the dark night, we recognize that obedience is only that upon which we can depend. Thus, obedience to God's leading is really the direction we should be traveling. Obedience is the only way we will ever regroup. Our tripartite parts know how to regroup when obedience becomes our direction. The scripture tells us what signs we should look for in the right direction. In 1 John 1:7, it says, "But if we walk in the light as He Himself is in the light, we have fellowship with one another, and the blood of Jesus, His Son, cleanses us from sin." Galatians 5:16 says, "But I say, walk by the spirit, and you will not carry out the desire of the flesh." In 2 Corinthians 5:7, it says, "for we walk by faith, not by sight." Here are three signs identifying the right direction for your journey:

1. The light is the sign of divine knowledge.
2. The Spirit is the sign of divine energy.
3. The faith is the sign of divine courage.

Look for Signs

There are signs of change. We must see the signs as the changes occur in the directions. Change is the dynamics of Creation. Thus, we need to look for signs of divine knowledge, energy, and courage. Everything in Creation is in a state of flux. Flux is the churning of Creation at the very core. This creative force is also at work in us. Affection, as you know is desire; however, desire is not evil as such. Nevertheless, it can become evil, just as anything, when used for evil purposes. We must desire to want to do the will of God. Earlier, we went down by the riverside to discover our positive affections. When we discovered positive affections to be good for our direction in life, we also discovered the direction of our journey beyond the riverside. Everything, at the core of Creation, is undergoing change simply as an adjustment in direction. Remarkably, adjustment in direction is the natural order of things. The state of becoming is constant change. Human beings are also in continuous creative change. For this reason, it is necessary to know our right direction. It is important to pause here to remember that wholeness is freedom and identity. In this sense, it is good to realize that the concepts of motion and stationary are incompatible concepts. The concept of motion can never become the concept of stationary, neither can the concept of stationary become the concept of motion at least not at the same time. Wholeness is always the result of motion. Therefore desire for wholeness is energy for change. Our desire for wholeness is the God beyond God pulling us along the path in which we travel, when it is the right direction.

The symbolic elements of Light, Spirit, Faith, and Change are symbols of wholeness. The symbols point the way to wholeness, freedom, and identity. We perceive the symbols in the sights and sounds of our environments. The symbols influence the affections. They mold and shape our mind, we can master these symbols. When we master the symbols, we will have mastered the secret of being. Learn the secret of being, by learning to master the symbols as the affections. Moreover, always remember that all behavior is learned and that affections are learned behavior, as well. That which is learned can always be unlearned. Nevertheless, unlearning a thing is more difficult than learning it. Therefore, we travel the pathway of the Via Negativa to unlearn behavior by letting go and letting be. Moreover, traveling the pathway of the Via Negativa is learning even if we are unaware. The teacher on the path is the Creator and the judge. We, therefore, learn the right way by using the symbols of change. Our ability to make the right decisions helps us to master the symbols in our head. We choose some affections and we let other affections go. Therefore, in the pathway of the Via Negativa, we learn that using symbols of change we master our affections within the sphere of time. More importantly, we learn the practical use of time in the right direction.

Time is Our Sphere in Eternity

When we are going in the right direction, we learn the practical use of time. Time is a variable of measurement. Time measures duration and distance. The more time used, the longer the duration, and the greater the distance. Conversely, the less time used the shorter the duration and the distance. While time is a human reality, it is nevertheless, a useful tool. On the other hand, eternality is void of time. We can be both in eternity and in time, at the same instance. However, time is strictly our sphere, while eternity is strictly God's sphere. We must deal first with the problem of eternity and time when we are dealing with our directions. If our direction presupposes a time factor, then we are traveling in a path that will lead to an end. However, if our directions presuppose an eternal factor, then it will constantly lead to new beginnings. Forward motion is linear. Some people think of time in circular motion and others think of time in linear motion. The concepts have a great influence on our worldviews. The important thing to know is if the direction is linear or circular. In Incarnation Centered Spirituality, the direction is linear motion. Think of this as if you are traveling in space. If you are going in circles, you will not experience anything new. However, if you are traveling in a straight line, new things will always appear. Space is the medium through which we travel. Space is physical, psychological, or spiritual. We cannot get outside of space, but we can measure the distance that we have traveled in space. This is important because space, time, and motion can be a simultaneous experience. When we are going in the same direction as linear time, in the direction of wholeness, then we are in eternity, even while in man-made time. We are moving out from our brokenness. Out, as opposed to up, is the only direction we can travel in spiritual space. This is true because we are always at the center of the universe. Wherever you are, you are at the center of the universe. We must always be moving out, in order to leave completely behind us, things that prevent our wholeness. Linear motion is the right direction to wholeness. We learn this in time, along the path to wholeness.

Your Direction is Already Inside of You

All behavior is learned. We learn that spiritual knowledge comes with birth and that other knowledge comes from the world. Spiritual knowledge is deep in the center of our inner self. Therefore, we should always live from our center. When we journey inward, we discover knowledge of our true self. What keeps us from discovering our true self is our belief that our false self is the true sphere of knowledge. We must realize that we do not learn spiritual knowledge from the world. Our spiritual knowledge is total inner knowledge; we do not learn spiritual knowledge from the world. This means our direction for inner knowledge must be inward. Moreover, our spiritual journey is always inward. This is so because what we seek is already within our true self. What you seek is at the divine point in you, where God becomes you. It is the point that remains unchanged in the midst of change. It is where you learn how to change into who you are fundamentally. It is to do what Jesus taught, when He says, "Go into your room and shut the door [Matthew 6:6]." The room is the interior. The inward journey is to the innermost center of divinity.

Moreover, you are always the center of the universe because God is at the center of your being. Remember that wherever you go and whatever you do, you are the center of the universe. You are the point where God is the ground of your being. Thus, the divinity of your life flows from the center in concentric circles. This concentric perspective is the idea of expanding circles of the inner self. This is a useful concept when we do not confuse it with linear motion in the path of wholeness. Concentric circles are evidence of expanding force of the inner self. When we are fulfilling our purpose in life, our influence expands in concentric circles, like a smooth lake that has been disturbed by a rock. We grow in influence when we move toward wholeness. The right direction moves us towards our interior. We must avoid the direction that holds us in a circular path.

Divine Will is from the Center

Essentially, your will is always part of the direction. Moreover, your will is from the center and is always operating in your life. The will operates as your very behavior in life. Better still, your will is your direction. So, when your will becomes God's will, you have solved your affection problems. Affection is the main problem in our life. We have two choices, either we can follow our will, or we can follow God's will. Satan uses our will to disobey the will of God. Our will is always in a fallen state, in the false self. The false self is what the Scripture calls flesh. We can never do what God wants us to do, until we are in the will of God. When we are in the will of God, we are traveling in the same direction as God, and from the same center as God. Anything outside the will of God is a rejection of God. God's will is the perfect idea about anything in our life. It is perfect because God is perfect. This may astound you, but God knows what we are supposed to be doing in this world. God's will make things happen in our lives that are always in our best interest. This is why we must constantly seek to make our affections God's will.

Affection, as we have seen, is a powerful force in human life. Affections motivate us to achievement. Affections, in fact, become our North Star. Affection or desire, keeps us moving until we accomplish what we are trying to accomplish. Faith, as we have seen in the right direction, is the substance of our affections. We believe strongly that we can achieve what we can conceive.

This is why faith is so important in your journey toward wholeness. It is faith that makes wholeness our possibility. Moreover, God's calling determines our affections. Incidentally, the call of God, the will of God, our affection, and our direction are the same. The right direction is our calling. Our calling is our path. We are traveling a direction in life because it is our calling. What we are seeking is seeking us. Our calling presses hard on our sense of total self. We find no rest until we reach the direction of our calling. Therefore, our affections become our direction.

Affections are essential to the direction of our journey. We never find our direction in life, until we find our essential affections for life. Moreover, our affections always point us in the direction of the light, the Spirit, the faith, and the courage leading us to our destiny. The pathway of the Via Negativa is the direction that we travel, in order to let go of all our negative affections.

Wholeness for the African American journey is freedom, justice and identity. Freedom is deeper than liberation and identity is more than just being different. Freedom is detachment and identity is uniqueness. Therefore, direction is the complete experience of freedom and identity. Affection for wholeness is the essential state of existence for following the pathway of the Via Negativa. We find the strength to be what we are because we are sure of our direction. The direction that we are traveling is the way of silence. Look for the silence. Silence is much more than quietness. Think of silence as the state of stillness so your inner self can hear the eternal voice of Creator God. Recognize that prayer is not effective until it is part of the silence. Do not, just talk to God in prayer, also listen to God. When we are just talking to God, we will never know what God is saying. You already know that it takes two to converse. So then, understand, prayer is a conversation with God. The goal of wholeness through Incarnation Centered Spirituality is the supernatural state of contemplation. Contemplation is constant listening to God. Listening to God is always putting us in contact with the divine center. God is always in the center of our being. God has never left us. The divine presence of God is part of our being. Remember, your direction is always inward.

We entered the Path of the Via Negativa to learn positive affections. Positive affection loves our cross in life. There is a cross, in the right direction, that each of us must bear in life. Our love of the cross is our inner will. The cross makes us whole. The positive affections of our inner will, to love the cross of Christ, keeps us moving in the right direction. However, if we bear a cross for our own benefit, we are going in the wrong direction. Our inner will connects us to the cross when we bear it as our exterior purpose in life. Your purpose in life makes you the person you are supposed to be. It is only when we are being who we are supposed to be, that we are being whole. Our journey is seeking our cross in life and bearing it as an act of obedience to the Creator who seeks us in life. Seeking our cross is the direction that leads us to our divine center. Cross seeking therefore, is the life of meditation. Ask God to show you the way through your prayer of meditation. More about meditation in the pathway of the Via Negativa follows to be learned in Chapter 7.

Chapter 7

Clearing the Mind of Foggy Thinking

I'm troubled, I'm troubled,
I'm troubled in mind in mind, if Jesus
Don't help me I sho'ly will die.

The enslaved singers of this Negro spiritual, "I'm Troubled In Mind," declare that the only help for the troubled in mind is Jesus. "If Jesus don't help me," they sang, "I sho'ly will die." Therefore, just as one needed to learn the direction down by the riverside, one must also develop a prayer life of meditation to clear one's mind of foggy thinking, as you follow your direction from the riverside. This requires that an individual develop an effective life of prayer; this is the prayer of meditation. Meditation helps you to clear your mind of foggy thinking. Your prayer of meditation becomes your vocation.

Vocation in Incarnation Centered Spirituality is your commitment of living according to the calling of God. This vocation is a life of repentance sustained by the prayer of meditation. The prayer of meditation is the balanced way to finding your true self. The balanced prayer of meditation is between the prayer of the mind and the prayer of the heart. The prayer of the mind is a reflective meditation of intellectual thought about the teachings of scriptures. The prayer of the heart is in-depth meditation that attempts to go into your innermost self, where as in repentance; you turn from your false self in order to find your true self. Each individual stays on task in the vocation of repentance with a clear mind through meditation of the head and of the heart. Meditation in its truest form is a life of prayer. When an individual is in a life of prayer, the individual is also in the vocation of prayer. The heart is the seat of one's being so it is in the heart where one really lives. The Scripture says, "as he thinketh in his heart so is he [Proverbs 23:7]." The heart is, also, the place of silent listening to the voice of God.

It is in this inner center where the presence of God is always actively speaking to each person. You must make the meditation of your heart an active practice, if you are to hear the voice of God, as well as, discover your true self. It is in the silence where the Spirit takes over. As F. C. Happold points out, the goal of the prayer of the heart is to draw as close as possible to that state of doing nothing and just looking. "This type of prayer is called the Prayer of Simplicity and Simple Regard."[11] The Prayer of Simplicity and Simple Regard is "the state of prayer in which the mind becomes more and more stilled, thought and reflection cease to be predominate elements, and words, concepts and symbols gradually fade away."[12] Mind prayer of meditation is also an act of listening to the voice of God through the thinking process. The prayer of the mind takes place at the level of thought. It is mental prayer. The prayer of the mind is a rational effort to transform the one who prays. The analysis in mind prayer is always an important part of the prayer of meditation. Take for instance; when we think about Incarnation Centered Spirituality analytically, we realize that while the Word of God became flesh, in further analysis we realize that the Incarnation is still taking place in us. The Word is still becoming flesh in us. The creative power of the Word still shapes life. This is why you must keep your mind on your vocation.

Keeping your mind on your vocation is the prayer of single-mindedness that results from the balanced meditation of the prayer of the mind and the heart. We need to master this balanced way of prayer of the mind and the heart. This balance is the ability to will one thing. Thus, we must learn to concentrate on God with a mind that stays on the Word of God. The best way to master meditation is by developing the art of single-mindedness. Internal life and external life are always compatible. The internal state of self, as we have seen, determines the external state. We control external life by controlling the internal state of self. This is extremely important to African Americans because we are living in an environment that judges us by our external appearance. In this racist society, the color of the skin matters. Therefore, you must raise your consciousness to the level you need in order to rise above the deception of Western man who tries to prove that you are inferior in order to hide his own inferiority. This art of meditation is really consciousness directed above White supremacy. Your meditation of single-mindedness is the ability to control your consciousness. It is the prayerful act of choosing your own mindset.

Meditation Is Thinking God's Thoughts

As we have learned, your thought is really your way of encountering the Mind of God. When we are thinking, it is always on two different levels. Either we are thinking on the level of our own thoughts or we are thinking on the level of God's thoughts. When you are thinking God's thoughts, you

are in your inner self where you make contact with God. Therefore, scripture is, also, necessary for encountering the Mind of God. Scripture primes
your mind with the rich wisdom of God. When you read and meditate on
the Scripture, you are in direct contact with God. This contact with God is
always on an intellectual level. We are always thinking and talking with the
spirit world. This requires watchfulness because Satan is also, in the spirit
world. This is why we must make sure we are always contacting the Mind
of God. Prayer makes contact with God, which is the ultimate encounter.
When we pray, as we have already seen, we are in direct contact with God.
Encountering the Mind of God is the contact of our mind with the same
eternal wisdom of God that keeps the universe on course and in existence.
You recognize the controlling Word of God.

Control is essential to concentration. Therefore, you must master the art
of concentration, which is consistent with meditation. If you can conceive it,
you can achieve it. Concentration is staying centered. This is why we must
master the art of concentration. As you have learned, we have a great wisdom
on the inside of us. You choose how and what you will think. This is what
makes singled mindedness important. What we see in the world is what we
call our "outsight." It is important to distinguish between the insight and the
outsight because one is the product of the other. Our single-mindedness is
also our insight. Insight means that we are in control of our inner life as we
control our thoughts. This is why we must master concentration. We must
keep an eye on our insight. It is our insight that makes our "outsight" what
it appears to be. As you have learned, we have a great wisdom on the inside
of us. This is why we must stay centered. Concentration is staying centered.
Our expectation operates out of our center. When we expect something in
life, it is because we have already formulated the concept in our minds, when
our minds grasp an idea it will produce that idea. This is why mastering the
art of concentration is essential in meditation. When you have control of
your mind, you also have control of your thoughts. Insight produces outsight.
Outsight is a matter of the focus on your calling because you can see where
you should be focused.

Focus is Concentration

Focus is your concentration on your calling. This concentration is the essence of meditation. Concentration is the ability to focus on one thing at a
time. Concentration refers to that which "has a common center, or is moving
toward a center and is best expressed by the term one-pointedness."[13] It all
starts with the calling. Calling, as we have seen, is really our vocation in life.

For this reason, our focus in life is on our ultimate purpose in life. Observation helps to keep us in our calling. When we stay alert, we are always aware of where we are in life as it relates to our calling. This is why focus is so important. Pure thought is always about our focus in life. Our ultimate purpose in life will always come down to our focus in life. What is life without a focus? When life is without focus, you need to center it. Therefore, it is important to know that we arrived in the world with a program. We call this program our predisposition. However, it is really the DNA in your cells. As an individual, you should remember that the program is always your calling for life trying to become visible in your life. This is why your focus in life is your ultimate purpose for life. Your purpose is just waiting for you to realize its presence. Your spiritual practice of meditation is how you can release it by your focus.

Furthermore, your inner life is very important for your journey in life because it possesses your real focus for life. Therefore, you must first get in contact with your inner life before trying to understand your external life. Meditation is the inward journey. We form our outside by what we discover on our inside. Your true self is on the inside influencing the outside. The false self is on the outside trying to influence your inside. It is the battle between the two selves, the true self and the false self, that determines the way your journey in life will go. This is why Incarnation Centered Spirituality is necessary for staying on your purpose. Your purpose in life always leads to your wholeness in life. This makes it necessary for you to get your affection under control. Consequently, your affection is the real struggle between the two selves. Your affections will master you if you do not master them. Your affections get in the way of your thinking. In fact, your affection is the product of your thinking. Therefore, it is important to think about your thinking. Essentially, meditation controls your thinking. You can rediscover your true self in meditation as you become more aware of your thinking.

Become aware of your reverie. The reverie is that stream of thought that floats beneath your thoughts. We all must learn how to control the reverie before we can control the art of meditation. We must learn how to let it just float on by without reacting to it. Inner thought is a big part of the meditation process and if we cannot get a handle on the daydreaming and musing that creep into our meditation, we will have a struggle with staying single-minded. Understandably, solitude is an important part of meditation. Solitude is the place where we are alone with God even in a crowd. We must realize that God is always with us. However, the problem is that we are not always in a solitary place with God. When we are with God in a solitary way, we are in a better condition to think about thinking. Metacognition is one word to express this concept of thinking about your thinking. This discussion, however, is more of an analysis of thinking about the thinking of God in His written Word. Meditation, as stated before, is the art of thinking about our thinking. Therefore this is the meditation of the mind and the heart. So, simply put, thinking about thinking is an inner journey. We find true solitude in our inner self.

The inner self is the place where we enter to be alone with God. It is the place that Teresa of Avila, a spiritual writer in the 16th Century, called the "Interior Castle." It is the place where God dwells. Rowan Williams recognized that Teresa of Avila was actually saying that the image of the Interior Castle was an "attack on interiority as an ideal in itself."[14] In order that we do not mistake the inner journey as an end in itself, we use the image of the inner hut. It is our hut. When we enter into the depths of our inner hut, we are in the dwelling place of God where we can see radiating love from the center of our self. It is here where we find our solitary place to listen to God. The inner hut is not a hiding place; it is a place of change. This is where we undergo a change from our inner self when we experience the out pouring love of God. This is where we recognize, after seeing the love of God, that there must be a change of self. This change results from our prayer life. Change of self is more important than knowledge of self. We are undergoing Incarnation. Our Incarnation is the Word becoming flesh in our earthly life. The study of God's Word makes our Incarnation solid. We study not because we are trying to learn any new thing, but rather, we are trying to verify what we already know in our inner self. In African American spirituality, the image of the inner hut is more conducive to the perception of our worldview.

Your Open Perception is Limitless

We want to be able to perceive as far as we possibly can. Limitless perception is the focused perception that we strive for in our meditation. Our imagination really determines our limitations. Furthermore, we need clarity. Thus, clarity is a goal of our meditation. We need to perceive clearly. Ultimate reality is a perception of what is fundamental truth beyond the apparent appearance of things. This perception is the ultimate reality of the Creator's presence. When we can see the presence of the Creator, we are then operating with an opened perception. The Bible verse, "Blessed are the pure in heart for they shall see God [Matthew 5:8]" is a practical statement. The pure in heart is also single-mindedness. When we focus our thinking, by concentrating on our calling, our ultimate purpose, and continuous meditation, with a pure heart, we will see the "heavens" opened in every situation of our life. Therefore, the result of focusing your thinking is about finding your purpose.

It is All About Your Purpose

Your spiritual journey begins and ends with a purpose. Therefore, when you are on a journey it is necessary to check your purpose along the way, to see if you are still on the right purpose. The value of meditation is its ability to keep you focused on your purpose. Meditation, also, helps you to reexamine your journey. The reexamination of your journey is necessary for thinking both about purpose and process. Both the purpose and process must be, as they ought to be if your journey is to remain true to your calling. Meditation helps you to check the relationship between the purpose and the process in your life. This relationship is the best way to determine if you are on your right path to wholeness. On the Path of the Via Negativa, the tool of Meditation helps you to stay in the right direction of detaching from negative affections as you journey toward wholeness. If there is a conflicted relationship between purpose and process, you are on the wrong path. You must recheck your initial point of departure. The initial departure is your ultimate start because you are always bound to the initial beginning of anything. Our practice of the prayer of meditation also keeps us in a checking mode. If there are any changes needed in the journey, then our meditation will make a correctional check between purpose and process.

Incarnation Centered Spirituality is rooted in the proper kind of meditation. We have authority to make the kinds of changes we need to make. Even though God leads us, we have authority to readjust the goals of our journey because we are ultimately responsible for our journey. God does not take away our responsibility in life. The Creator makes us responsible for this stewardship of life in the beginning. The originality of your journey is important; however, your responsibility for your journey is most important. We are even responsible for the originality of our journey. The originality of your journey is your prayer of meditation. This is your prayer life. You possess the original blueprint of your course in life. There is nothing else in the world like your original purpose. Moreover, in your prayer life, the signs of your journey are always along your path, for you to check and see if you are still on the right purpose and process. There were signs of your path in life even when you were born. However, you are responsible for taking your own path. God will call you to your path, but God will not make you take your path. This is a good thing to remember when you celebrate your birthday. This celebration is really a time to check the purpose and the process of your birth.

Meditation is important because, as we have said, thinking generates your emotions. We can always change the way we feel by changing the way we think. There is no way to change your feelings, in this case feelings are what we are calling affections, except by changing your thinking or your actions. This is really, what mortification means for the self. When we change the thinking and the feelings change we are really mortifying our affections. Mortification is a need that grows out of our detachment from desires that affect our soul. Our affections for things apart from God are so damaging to our soul that there is a need for mortification. Mortification is the act of "hating, conquering, and killing the impulses and habits which keep us from God; and of wrenching ourselves away from all circumstances which are for us occasions of sin."[15] Thoughts of mortification have a power of their own. They have the ability to make things change. This is why we must always be in control of our thoughts. In our meditation, we let affection go through the process of dying. Dying is the process of death. Death is a noun while dying is a verb. This simply means that, in mortification, the feelings that seek to control our behavior are in the process of dying. Furthermore, mortification is also the process of thoughts dying that control our feelings. This is why there is a mortification of the self at the conscious level of meditation. Do not underestimate the power of meditation. God inspires and illuminates us through our meditation.

Always keep this in mind, God inspires us through our prayer life of meditation. Inspiration is the result of the inbreathing of the Spirit of God. The input of the Spirit of God inspires us. This inspiration is not motivation. The power of God gives us inspiration but we motivate ourselves. Motivation is produced by our own action. Enthusiasm is also the inbreathing of God. However, it is the direct inbreathing of God for zeal. While inspiration can come from the environment around us, it is always the act of God. We may see something that inspires us to go to another level in life. Enthusiasm, on the other hand, is the energy of God that keeps us going. Affection is the force that motivates the forward motion of our journey. We take the journey in life because our affection awakens the idea and the need to seek our desires. When we embraced the Incarnation, a spark of divine love came alive in our inner self. It was our love of God and our love of man for God's sake. It was, in fact, the illumination of the great commandment; "to love the Lord thy God with all thy heart, and with all thy soul, and with all thy mind, and with all thy strength: this is the first commandment. And the second is this; Thou shalt love thy neighbor as thyself. There is no other commandment greater than these [Mark 12:30-31]." This is the ignition of the divine spark in the Image of God in the innermost part of your being. You did not receive this Image by anything you have done. It has always been there from the creation of man just waiting to be ignited. You experienced the ignition when you embraced the Incarnation. This is what started you on your journey to wholeness. Thus, meditation will protect you as you journey.

Meditating on the Word of God protects us from our false thinking. This deception is a great danger on your journey. Our own thinking will mislead us if we are not careful. Satan always works on our thinking. Satan knows that our mind and heart operate together influencing each other. This is how he tries to deceive us in our thinking. Influence is what we must always be aware of because everything is trying to influence us. We must permit ourselves to be influenced only by the forces that help us to make our journey to wholeness. Therefore, we must choose to let the Word of God become our thinking. It is important to remember that the goal in the art of meditation is the ends must justify the means. You, in the finally analysis, are the only person responsible for your journey. Your first responsibility to yourself on your journey, is reflective meditation on the Word of God. Moreover, you are responsible for maintaining the simple regard needed for your meditation.

Ultimate Reality is Your Ground of Being

Meditation is also seeking the Ground of Being. Since God is Ultimate Reality. The Ultimate Reality is the Ground of Being. Seeking the Ground of Being for rebuilding your self, in the real sense, is what it means to seek Ultimate Reality. The Ground of Being for rebuilding our own lives is the reality of truth. Reality is what ought to be rather than what should be in life. Thus, there is always an ethical dimension to reality. This ethical dimension is what makes what ought to be your ultimate reality. Originality is another way of saying reality. Originality is what will always be when everything else has passed away. Truth, therefore, is the basic element of the Ground of Being. Truth is originality. We meditate on the truth when we meditate on the Word of God. In our meditation, we perceive that Truth and the Word of God are the same. Seeking the Ground of Being for rebuilding our lives is the journey of Incarnation Centered Spirituality. Thus, seeking is an inward journey. This is why meditation is a vital part of the journey. Your prayer life of meditation is your movement towards complete union with the God beyond God. It is your victory in a broken world. In Chapter 8, we will see how to gain victory over this present age of deception and violence. This is the age where the belief in religion has replaced the belief in Jesus Christ as our personal Savior. Victory is your ability to reverse deception and violence and return to your belief in Jesus Christ as your personal Savior. In Chapter 8, you will learn how to use the tool of Victory with the technique of Affection in the Path of the Via Negativa.

Chapter 8

Overcoming Life's Struggles Today

Until I reach-a ma home, until I reach-a my home,
I nevah inten' to give de journey oveh until,
I reach-a my home.

The enslaved African American understood the meaning of victory. In the Negro spiritual, "Until I reach-a Ma Home," they declared that they intended to stay on their journey to victory. They knew that victory is in staying on the path of their journey to wholeness. Victory is the proof that we have retained our belief in Jesus Christ as our personal Savior rather than having replaced it with a belief in religion. "Positive" is the essential test results of the proof of temptation in the spiritual journey you take in life. In other words, your spiritual journey should result as positive when tested for temptations. If there is no temptation in your spiritual journey, then it is the wrong journey. In fact, temptation is a source of the victory. Victory means, after all, and this is common sense when we stop to think about it, that you have overcome struggles. Affections attract temptations. Temptation is the other side of affection. All affections bring their own brand of temptations. For every yes, there is a corresponding no. It helps us to understand that affection is like the ignition of a spark of fire from friction. Friction comes from resistance. Next, the spark must have something to ignite. Affection is the material ignited by the spark of temptation. Additionally, if this temptation is not extinguished it can consume you totally. This is why temptation is a source of victory. Victory is, after all, that which must be, in spite of everything else we do in life, if we are to be an overcomer in life. The religion of Jesus is about overcoming our sin nature. Your temptations in life are necessary, if there is to be a struggle for your self-development. For without the struggle, there can be neither growth nor victory.

Your Faith Is Your Defense

Faith is the internal force that defeats temptation. It is the first line of defense against external forces. When we have faith, we have the power to see in a different way. The Scripture teaches that, "faith is the substance of things hoped for, the evidence of things not seen [Hebrews 11:1]." We can see things through the eyes of faith that are invisible to the natural eyes. Hope is substance that faith validates. Love also operates through faith. This trinity of faith, hope, and love makes a powerful force against temptation. When we find ourselves face to face with temptations in life, all we have to do is remember that faith is the thing already done, and hope is the thing that is always expected. Supernatural love is the force that continually helps us to act believing that our actions have the backing of God. Love helps us to see beauty in life and in people, in such a way that we have the power to keep on hoping.

Facing the evils in life with faith is, also, your first line of battle against Satan himself. Satan uses the voice of your false self, which is always contrary to your true self. Moreover, when we see the world through the false self we are looking at the Great Impostor's lies. Resisting the voice of the false self and false perceptions becomes a personal fight against the Impostor's deceptions. When we use our ability to resist Satan's lies, then we can look at life through the eyes of our true self. This is why you have been trying to enter into your true self. The ability to control your thinking is the beginning of the defeat of Satan. Your thinking makes your feelings a force in your life that causes you the most trouble. It is through your feelings, where your powerful affections dwell, that Satan attacks you with false notions in life, which causes most of your fears and makes you, act and feel the way you do.

Courage Is Acting Through Your Fears

Courage is the ability to face our fears. When we recognize our fears, we must then have the ability to face the fears, if we are ever going to move on in life. Wisdom helps us to know that fear is the absence of faith. For faith is the opposite of fear. Once we recognize our fears, we have gained the victory over our fears. The fear of death is our greatest fear because it prevents us from doing the things in life that we ought to do. We, who practice Incarnation Centered Spirituality however, do not fear physical death. The idea of not existing is what causes the most fear. However, when we face the fear of death, we become aware of the fact that death is not annihilation. Then we know why it is necessary to recognize our fear. This becomes the open door to our victory. There is no victory in life until you first face your fears. When you face your fears then you are prepared to do battle with life. We remember that supernatural love keeps us in perfect peace. We make creative contact with the supernatural love that we received at our conversion on the Path of the Via Negativa using the technique of Affection, and the tool of Victory. This supernatural love replaces your negative affections for the world with the desire to become a co-creator with God. You begin to understand how perfect love casts out fear. You began to realize that your self-centeredness causes your fear [1 John 4:18]. Supernatural love leads us to the recognition of our self-centeredness. When we recognize this, then we are aware that doubt is self-centered behavior. Self-centeredness makes you focus on your own self. Faithlessness is the bag that you are left holding when you doubt God's love for you. It is your doubt that reveals that you are relying on your own power in life, instead of relying on the power of God. At this point, the possibility of your wholeness reveals its beautiful head for the first time. Now you realize that doubt is the greatest act of self-centeredness. You have replaced the self for God. You are trusting in self instead of trusting in God. It is necessary that we learn that doubt is self-centeredness. Then we can begin trusting God more and the self less.

Strike the Beast First

The beasts in front of us are the negative affections, such as hatred, jealously, greed, gluttony, and others we met on the Path of the Via Negativa. The affections that would separate us from God are the beasts in our path. Immediately we have to slay this beast in front of us. We must act at this very moment. If we miss this moment, we miss the opportunity to slay the beast in front of us. Having a well-planned strategy is the way we defeat the beast in front of us. We must have an operational strategy prepared before encountering the beast. If we wait until the moment the beast attacks us, to plan our strategy to slay the beast, then it is too late. If we must retreat, it means that we are not prepared to face the beast. We must be sure that beast in front of us is slain. We can never move on in life until we slay the beast confronting us in our pathway to wholeness. We must slay the beast in front of us otherwise, we will have to fight the beast repeatedly. We can put the fight off as long as we want, but until we defeat the beast in front of us, we will never be able to advance in life.

The beast in front of us is what keeps us from moving on in our journey. If apples are your weakness, do not wait until you are in an apple grove before you plan the strategy to overcome apples. To do so is pure arrogance. Arrogance is the attitude that keeps us from recognizing our own nothingness. When we recognize our own nothingness then we will develop the beneficial attitude of humility. We will get rid of our arrogance by developing the affection for only God. Affection for God only removes this barrier of pride that keeps us from overcoming the forces in our path. We shall overcome because we plan our strategy for spiritual war against our negative affections with the help of God. God empowers us to see beyond our deficiencies. Our enemy hides from us. We do not really see the enemy lurking in the darkness. We have no chance to defend ourselves from the enemy if we cannot see that the enemy of affection is trying to defeat us, as we journey along the Path of the Via Negativa. Ignorance in this case can be costly. When we do not know what to watch out for we are unable to prepare a strategy. Usually it is too late to plan when life has caved in around us. Mystery is the thing that we have before us but we cannot understand the nature of mystery until it is too late. This is why bringing the possibility of defeat by our affections out into the open is the wisest thing to do. You begin your strategy by dealing with your affections. Affection is a real danger in your path. Affection can be an unknown enemy. If you are unaware of your affections then you may be putting more energy into a part of your life than you should. This is why some kind of asceticism is necessary in the spiritual journey. Detachment is necessary. We must let some of our affections go. We have to be in control of our affections. Our affections are very important to our aspiration in life since our affections influence our lives even more than our intellect. Control of your affection in the spiritual journey becomes the spiritual discipline that is decisive for your victory over Satan. This is why self-knowledge is indispensable for victory over affections.

Pilgrim Know Thyself

The knowledge of self is indispensable since individuality is a strong part of your journey. Individuality helps you to determine who you are in a world of deception. It is very essential to know who you are for a large part of your victory is the rediscovery of your identity. The spiritual journey of Incarnation Centered Spirituality is the vehicle that helps you to rediscover your individuality. It leads you into solitude with God. Solitude is your natural mode in life on this journey. When we develop our lifestyle of solitude, we are developing the ability to understand that aloneness is distinct from loneliness.

Wholeness is the ability to be alone without being lonely. On the other hand, loneliness is actually what is unnatural. No one should ever have to feel lonely. Instead, you could be whole. Moreover, wholeness is the ability to strive for your individuality and to do it in a way that you are in a safe place or sanctuary that feeds your true self. Knowledge of your true self is what you should strive to possess. This knowledge of your true self is essential for guidance. Guidance is an internal process that comes with the inner working of the Holy Spirit. On this spiritual journey, we need the guidance of the Holy Spirit. When we yield to the Holy Spirit, we are yielding to the guidance that is necessary to help us along the journey to wholeness. We, therefore, must be aware of our own individuality. Remember God works through the person who has knowledge of self. Energy is always in the guidance of the Holy Spirit. The energy to rise above your circumstances in life is what helps you to develop a winning strategy. Intelligence comes automatically when the Holy Spirit is guiding us. The Mind of God leads us in our journey, when we are yielding to the Holy Spirit. Yielding to the Holy Spirit is the only winning strategy we have in this life against our defeating affections. Hence, we must know who we are, but more than this, God must be working with whom he created us to be. Knowing our identity is the only way we can take a stand in life. Our stance is an important part of the defense that we have when fighting a battle with a strong enemy. The stance we take in life gives us the flexibility we need for positioning ourselves in the right place with the right posture. The stance must have bounce in it. Bounce is the ability to spring up and away from our opponent. This bounce is only possible when we are on our toes. We must always be on our spiritual toes. If you are ever caught standing flatfooted, you are open to a strong blow to your vital parts. Just as stance is useful in allowing a dancer to shift weight in the direction that the dancer needs to go, it also gives you the flexibility to be prepared for the enemy seeking to destroy you. Your stance develops personal fortitude. This fortitude is the inner strength that helps us to defeat the enemy. If we are strong on the inside, then we are able to take on whatever the foe might be in our path. So, finding the balance of your own identity in life is a strategy for winning your fight against the forces seeking your destruction.

God Will Show You the Glory of Creation

The human being possesses a glory that no other animal possesses. This glory reveals itself in the mind. Moreover, inspiration has a great deal to do with our knowing the glory of our creation. Revelation is the only way we can know the glory of our creation. Our glory is a part of the Creation that Satan diminished when he deceived Adam and Eve in the garden. Every now and then, there is an inspiration that comes like a flicker of light flashing in our inner selves. We catch a glimpse of it but then it fades away. Imagination captures a quick sight of it passing into the darkness. When this imagination goes to work on our revealed glory, our aesthetic nature comes alive with colors, shapes, and sounds that make our aesthetic nature want to experience more of it. We know that there is more to our nature than the fallen state we experience daily. The yearning for a glory that our true self senses is the beginning of the restoration of this glory in our human nature. Your restoration begins in the inner silence of your true self.

Walk with your Angel

Silence helps us to walk with our ministering angels. Walking with our ministering angels becomes one part of our victory. In our spiritual journey, we are on the road to victory, when we recognize that we walk with our ministering angels, in our quiet solitary walk. Studying helps us to understand this solitary walk. On this solitary walk, we are able to study the sights and sounds that bombard us from all sides. Placing yourself in silence and solitude is an excellent method to walk and talk with your ministering angel. In this walk, you reclaim a faith that illuminates your path. Your reclaiming faith begins the process of reclaiming your sense of victory. When we reclaim our sense of victory, then we reclaim a new sense of power. Confidence then becomes more than just a brave front claiming a false security. It becomes a sense of power that goes beyond our own mortal power. You become awakened to the spiritual truth that divinity is far more than a religious doctrine grounded in the history books. Divinity becomes a spiritual reality in which to participate as part of our natural lives. The same divine power that was an integral part of the natural life of Jesus supercharges your own life. The act of reclaiming your sense of victory will infuse you with an awareness of new divine power in your life. The supernatural power of the Almighty God will empower you to complete your spiritual journey in life. The supernatural power of the Almighty God has in it a mysterious creative element. In Chapter 9, you will explore the technique of Generation of the Turner E.A.G.L.E. Technique in the Path of the Via Creativa, using the tool of Creation to rediscover your creative ability.

PATH III

THE VIA CREATIVA, USING YOUR GENERATIVE POWERS

Chapter 9

Remembering How to Be Creative

Wheel, oh wheel, wheel in de middle
In de middle of a wheel; wheel, oh wheel,
Wheel in de middle of a wheel.
Zekiel saw de wheel of time, wheel in de
middle of a wheel.
Every spoke was human kind, wheel in de
Middle of a wheel.

This Negro Spiritual reveals the remarkable imagination of the enslaved African American singers. They recognized that God is the greatest artist with an incomparable supernatural imagination. Moreover, these singers knew that the imagination of God is always at work in the Creation. In God, we have all the artistic designs and forms we will ever need in life to satisfy our aesthetic taste. We just need to look around at the sights and hear the sounds in our world of experience using the eyes of a spiritual artist. The human artist is unable to operate outside of the Mind of God. Just remember that Creation is all about imagination. The power of divine imagination is in human life because it was first in God. The greatest artistic imagination ever performed is the Incarnation. Incarnation is the greatest improvisation of divine mind in human history. The Incarnation is work done, with the thought of bringing a great bang from the orchestration of divine imagination. Incarnation occurred at just the perfect time to create a new humanity. This is why angels sang when Jesus was born in Bethlehem. What happened that morning in Bethlehem was not the beginning of the music of Incarnation. It was just a jazzy melody, an improvisation, of the celestial choir singing a medley of divine tunes, which already filled the universe. Creation is nothing more than the outworking of God's Mind. It is the manifestation of God's inner thoughts. This is the wonderful thing about creativity. Creativity is the conceptualization that the power of divine imagination is restorable in you. It all starts with the concept of Creation.

The word concept means to conceive. It suggests that there have been receptions of many bits and pieces of information. To understand the creative process, we need to understand this process of reception of information. Moreover, after the receptions, a perception is developed. Then a concept forms. Thus, concepts develop after a long process of receptions and perceptions. There are many things entering our minds everyday, but we are unaware of most of the things that are entering our minds. It is only after a long time of reception that we realize a perception is developing in our minds. Essentially, the mind is sensitive to what is inside the inner self. It is after the perceptions develop to some extent that you are aware of them, then, you must try to make sense out of them. Only then does the concept become apparent. For this reason, we cannot name the concept until it takes form in our mind. Our imagination helps us name it. Moreover, the name, which we give it, is the reflection of our imagination. Our creative ability manifests itself as our imagination in expressing concepts. Expression is necessary in the act of Creation. The first thing that God asked Adam to do was to exercise his ability to give expression to Creation. Naming concepts is expressing creation. You must name. This is why after the conception of the baby, comes the birth, then the naming.

You cannot create in a vacuum. Furthermore, in spirituality, we cannot name concepts until God asks us. Thus, we must cooperate with God in Creation. Cooperation is a spiritual responsibility for believers. You must remember that we create spiritually through the imagination of God. It is through the cooperation of believers that birthing is possible. Birthing is a spiritual responsibility for believers, because birthing is the very meaning of Creation. We are God's conduits. As you know, conduits perform the necessary work of passing things along to the place where they need to go for change and production. The believer is the conduit of Creation. Consistency, therefore, becomes clearer as we study it in Creation; it is the most important part of birthing. The believer is the one who the Spirit uses to continue the creative process of God. This is really why birthing is a spiritual responsibility for believers. Our most important creativity is in birthing justice, freedom, and peace in the Kingdom of God. These things come from a heart of divine love. In this discussion, we have been speaking about generating.

Generation or the generating process flows through a head full of imagination and a heart full of divine love. This kind of fullness is an important part of creativity. It is out of the fullness of the Creator that things come into being. The fullness of the innermost self is the heart where the Creator dwells. It is out of this heart that the Creator operates. God provides the creative substance. Therefore, substance is not a problem when there is a heart full of the Creator. By now, it is clear that we are all creators. God made us to be creators; however, this means more than just reproducing things. This means that we take the substance in our inner self and produce things that have not been made before. This is our own way of being original. Nature is the substance out of which we create. We cannot create nature, but we can create inspired by nature. This is what the phrase "out of the abundance of the heart" means. We speak it into being out of our inner self. Remember, it is out of the heart that the mouth speaks.

Speaking is creative. The straw in the field turns into mansions through speaking them into being. We have the power of speech to convert things into more things. Touching the straw can cause the straw to become bricks. When we know the power of the creative process, we can use the speech and touch to convert matter into energy, thereby changing into whatever kind of energy we need. The power of Creation is more than what we think in physical terms. Imagination is the most powerful part of the creative process. The imagination is the only limitation to the creativity. Straw in the field can be converted into mansions through the act of creation. When we use the power of Creation, then we take control of the process of evolution. By evolution, we mean the natural and spiritual unfolding process in Creation. Each believer has a unique gift for creating. Individuality is important. It is a creative necessity. By now, you must know your own individuality.

Individuality is the mandate in life to be your true self. This is important because this is how making it according to the plan initiated in the true life is possible. Everything about you is unique. Your uniqueness is a part of God's plan. You cannot produce uniqueness, if you are not first aware of your own uniqueness. The seed in the inner self is unique. The seed in your inner self must manifest in the Creation. And the seed can only be manifested if we discover the uniqueness that we already possess. The plan already exists in our inner self. We are the ones who have the only part to the rest of the Creation in our inner self. We must always be aware, that the plan was in our physical birth, just waiting to be born again. Spirituality is the discipline to explore our inner self and rediscover the seeds.

You must have a creative discipline. This discipline is an important skill to learn in order to become a whole person. Remember that wholeness is also holiness. Holiness is the New Testament understanding of becoming a whole person. It is clear that Jesus healed a lot of people who needed to be made whole. Jesus was able to heal broken people because He could see their brokenness. This takes a special kind of seeing. The technique of Generation in the Turner E.A.G.L.E. Technique develops the discipline to see. Discipline is important when it comes to visualization. Visualization is a developed skill of seeing. We must learn this skill. Perception is also important when it comes to visualization. Perception, too, is a certain kind of seeing. We are the perceiver and it is important to know that we can do whatever we want to do with our perception. Reception, on the other hand, is the influences that come into our mind even though we may not be aware of them. This is why visualization is a learned behavior on the journey to becoming a whole person. As we travel this journey, we learn to see in a unique way. We become aware that we see in both our sleeping and waking dreams. We, however, must learn to deal with our waking dreams. You must know when you are dreaming while awake.

The statement "Follow the yellow brick road," has a great deal to say about the power of our waking dreams. The dream is something that we associate with sleep. Therefore, it is important that we become aware that we have dreams while awake. In fact, the best of our creative energy occurs in our waking dreams. Following the dream while we are awake is like following the yellow brick road. We meet all kinds of people and experiences in this dream state. It is like being hypnotized. We are awake but yet we are dreaming of great things. You must be determined to develop the power of following the waking dreams. Determination makes the power of the waking dream easy to follow. When you are determined to see things through to their conclusions, you will realize the dream. You must believe that you can follow the waking dream to its creative conclusion. Your belief is also a part of the waking dream. When we believe that we can achieve something we will. This kind of mindset is what the think tanks do on a regular basis. When we know that we are awake while dreaming, we realize that we are able to move in a creative way toward birthing.

You may wonder why it is important to move toward birthing. It is important because dynamic is better than static. When we are dynamic, we are moving toward the goal of our journey. Remember, the creative process is part of the generation process. God is calling us to generate new things in the Creation. This is risk taking. However, learning is the beneficial part of risk taking that leads to new ways of understanding how old things work in a new way. We learn to collect impressions and images. Collection of impressions and images along the way will help you to create in a way that is really a useful way of our risk taking. There is more to most things than what meets the eye. So we have to be bold enough to take risks. We have to be willing to follow the impressions and images wherever they go, even though, it might be a dead end street. Nevertheless, we will be the richer for having taken the risk. Nothing ventured, nothing gained, is especially true in spirituality. In spirituality, we are on the hunt for meaningful ways to assimilate the raw materials that we discover on our journey. We, after all, are looking for our own divinity.

Searching for your divinity guarantees that you will meet help along the way. Divinity is the life that participates in the supernatural. In a life of divinity, nothing is ever impossible. In fact, our purpose is in our divinity. Furthermore, purpose is the real goal of life. Therefore, when we discover the divine purpose of our life we also discover the divinity of our life. We also find spiritual treasures in our search. Treasures are under every rock that we overturn. Overturning rocks is the substance of the search. We just have to have the faith to turn rocks over. It is the supernatural quality of life that makes it possible for help to be available everywhere. The most important thing to remember is that help is not always recognized. This, then is why, we must expect everything we meet to be our helper. When we expect everything we meet to be our help, we will be careful how we treat the things and people we meet along the way. Look for the images in people and things you meet. Everything is an image. Image is more than just a reproduction that represents something. It is the real indicator of what we have been taking into our minds. This is the most important learning about the technique of Generation.

With the technique of Generation, we become aware of our reception, perception, and conceptions in a new way. The processes are there so that we might look at them through the creative process. The law of reciprocity is always at work in our lives. Keep in mind that the Via Creativa is the path along which mind is differentiated. On this path, we discover the personal mind and the Universal Mind. There is a reciprocal relationship between your mind and God's Mind. Spiritual law requires that we always get back what we sow. Thus, the images are fruits of what we have sown in our minds. They are the reflections of our inner life. The reflections let us know what we have in our mind. We see the inner images that we have taken in from the outside. What you have in you comes out of you. This is the law of reciprocity in the creative mind. If we want to participate in the creative process in a way that will be effective, then we must spend some time shaping and exploring our minds. What goes in is what comes out. We must pay attention to our inner self.

Failure to pay attention to our inner self is dangerous. It can lead to the kind of self that has nothing in it but the monstrous and the smallness of a deficient inner self. You must discover the receptivity of the inner self as soon as possible. We must realize that we are receiving all the time. It is only when we are aware of this phenomenon that we are able to deal with it. Helplessness is sure to creep in if we don't take care of the inner self. The many images coming in from the world can confuse the inner self. This can cause the inner self to shutdown. The inner self will resort to helplessness. Helplessness is a learned behavior. Therefore, we must always expect a breakthrough. Expectation is the way we must operate in life. Moreover, expectation is a learned behavior. Since expectation is a learned behavior, you must develop the ability to expect the inner self to be alive with seeds of life. You should have discovered the receptivity of the inner self early in the journey. This lack of knowledge about the receptivity of the inner self will lead to poverty. You must know the inner self. You are looking for any signs of ingratitude. Ingratitude is a sure sign of the poverty of the false self, the ego-self. As we pointed out above creation comes from a rich inner self, pass the ego- self which is the false self.

Poverty, in many cases, is the result of the attitude of ingratitude. We become poverty-stricken when we lose the attitude of thankfulness. The lack of thankfulness is in the false self. We have learned to be unthankful as an attitude of life. We need to change our attitude to gratitude about life so we can move on at a higher altitude in life. Our attitude of gratitude increases our mental altitude; we can never rise above ungrateful thinking. As our thinking is void of gratitude, we are as the lower animals. The knowledge of the universal mind helps you to move above the level of lower animals. We learn to be thankful just as we learn the other things of importance in life. We learn to behave at higher altitudes because it is according to the way we perceive in life. Remember, our thinking conditions our affections. We learned to detach from affections that prevent us from loving God and loving man for God's sake.

Never forget that the affections have a powerful attraction. Affections attract whatever you want strongly enough. There is a supernatural law that determines the attraction of things. The supernatural law makes it possible in the realm of affections. Remember we are seeking beauty and truth as our wholeness. Our aesthetic affection is for beauty and truth. This desire for beauty and truth attracts the kind of urges we have for the creative life. This is how the power of attraction works in the creative process. Perfection is the outward expression of an inner affection for perfection. Because God is perfect, we seek perfection in our own inner self. The power of Godly affection results in our attraction for perfection. This Godly affection is the kind that all contemplative pilgrims possess.

Models of the contemplative pilgrims are in the history of the Church. In Christian Spirituality, the contemplative pilgrim established the standards for the Early Church handed down through the years. They were hearers of the sounds around them that made them aware of the creative force in the gospel. The same sounds come into our minds as we are traveling along the path to wholeness. The creative sounds make the difference in the life of the hearer. This is why contemplative pilgrims are still creative models in the world. They are our first teachers. The created effects have a long history. We are part of that history. It is our responsibility, if we are taking the journey of Incarnation Centered Spirituality along the five-fold path to wholeness, to come to the creative process, just as all spiritual masters have done down through history. We join the spiritual masters through faith. Learning to use faith is a necessary part of spiritual discipline. In the next chapter, Chapter 10, you will examine the steps to exercising your faith. You will also develop your understanding about the spiritual discipline of the tool of faith.

Chapter 10

Believing is More Than Just Thinking

O, by an' by, by an' by I'm gwinter lay down
My heavy load, O I know my robes
gwinter fit me well, I'm gwinter lay down
my heavy load, I tried it on at de gates of
hell I'm gwinter lay down my heavy load.

The enslaved creators of this spiritual, "By and By," believed that by and by they would lay down their heavy load. They believed that freedom, justice, and identity were achievable. Belief turns into faith when it leaves the head and enters the heart. "I tried it on," sings the slave, "at de gates of hell." Belief has become a reality at the gate of hell. Believing is more than just thinking. It is the power of generation. Generative thinking is faith. Faith is an essential part of this historical period. Faith is a tool of Generation in the Turner E.A.G.L.E. Technique for Incarnation Centered Spirituality. Faith generates; it is our assurance that God is working behind the scenes to honor our expectations. We sense this when we try to reach the goals that we have set for ourselves. The scripture teaches that faith is integrally connected to Christian Spirituality. We are told, "Now faith is the assurance of things hoped for, the conviction of things not seen. For by it the men of old gained approval [Hebrews 11:1-2]." On the Path of the Via Creativa, things just seem to happen without explanation. Some call the unexplained occurrences serendipitous events but on the journey of spirituality, they are providential events. There are times when just the right person shows up in our lives. This is why it is impossible to please God, if we do not depend on God for everything in our life. Hebrews 11:6 says, "And without faith it is impossible to please Him, for he who comes to God must believe that He is, and that He is a rewarder of those who seek Him." The dependency on God is the sure way of learning that God is working behind the scenes, but more importantly, it shows that you are honoring God. When we depend upon God, then God must produce what we are depending on God for. If it is the will of God, this dependency is the work of faith. There is a direct relationship between faith and dependency. This relationship causes the will of God to operate in our lives. Faith is obedience. Our obedience is the sure way of showing that we know God is working behind the scenes in our lives. It is behind the scenes because we cannot always see what God is doing. When we want to know what God is doing in our lives, all we have to do is obey God's will. Moreover, we can sense in our inner self that the hand of God is working behind the scenes. This is the distinction between faith and believing. Faith trusts while believing knows. Faith is a heart thing, while believing is a head thing. It must happen in the head first, before it can happen in the heart. Therefore, we must develop an intellectual concept of eternity.

As a result, of our intellectual concept of eternity, we sense that God is the only eternal being. We come to understand that there is nothing but nothing and the God beyond God. God is also a no thing and God cannot be a thing. This is because God is indescribable. Moreover, there can never be anything besides God. If there were anything else beside God in the beginning, then there is no way God could be the only eternal being. The fact that God is the only eternal being is the reason why, there must always be nothing but nothing. God uses nothing as the substance of Creation. The only thing that had substance in the beginning, was the Word of the God, beyond God. This is why faith is the substance of things expected. Moreover, substance is the Word of God. God created the universe out of the stuff of God's Word. However, we must understand that the Word of God is more than linguistics and verbal symbols. Man created linguistics and symbols in order to make sense of his environment. The Word of God is the energy behind Creation. The Word of God has the power to keep substance in existence. If the Word of God is not present in substance then substance disappears. We learn spiritual laws from physical laws. All substance is potential energy. Energy flows from one state to another. It is constantly changing into different forms of substance. Matter is energy.

The Matter of Creation is Energy

Science also confirms faith as energy. Physics is the science that deals with the physical property of the universe. The science of physics also deals with quantum particles. This branch of science studies the smallest particles of matter. Quark is the name of the particles that quantum physics deals with. However, thought can cause the quantum energy to shape itself according to thought. Our thoughts can affect the way nature reacts. Bear in mind that thought is also words. The point at which thought changes matter is the point in the Creation where the spiritual interacts with the physical. A spiritual force causes the quantum structure to react to thoughts. There is a relationship between our thinking and the actions of nature. Energy is the ultimate force of all matter. Everything is turning into energy. Therefore, everything is spiritual. Natural and Spiritual law are the same law. All laws have a law that governs them; this law is what Henry Drummond called the "Law of Continuity". This is the law of laws. There is a consistency in the universe that connects the spiritual world with the natural world. This is not a suggestion to practice nature worship. But, it is rather a strong suggestion that by faith you can transcend nature, by the Law of Continuity, as Jesus taught us, when He said, "Whatsoever a man thinks in his heart so is he." The heart, that place where the Spiritual Mind of God speaks to the spiritual mind of man, is the location of our thinking. Thus, Jesus calls attention to the mind.

Notice that Jesus says, "Whatsoever a man thinks in his heart." Jesus makes a distinction here between man's mind and God's Mind. There is the Universal Mind and the individual mind. The Universal Mind flows through our mind, but we do not always make the connection. We make the connection only through faith. Paul tells us that, "faith comes by hearing and hearing by the Word of Christ." The Word of Christ is the Mind of God. The Mind of God is the creative power flowing through us. Remember, there is mind first before there is wisdom, as evidenced by the fact that, all of Creation contains wisdom. What a wonderful truth! The great distinction between the Western concept of the Word and the African American concept of the Word is clear in the Negro Spirituals. Almost forgotten in the West, is the understanding of the Hebrew word "Dabhar." This Hebrew word Dabhar translated into the English language as a word misses the powerful concept of Dabhar as the creative energy--"Word" of God. We understand Dabhar best when we go back to the Genesis account of Creation and see the Dabhar at work. We have the Dabhar in us to use as a participant in Creation. We are always acting as the conduit of the creative power of God. We can have the power to take any thought we want for creative birthing. Thinking is all we have to do. Anything we can think of we can do. You are greatly helped with the birthing when you are aware that God's intention is the force behind the creative flow. The first intention that the universe experienced was the intention of God. Intention is the power behind all we do. Desire is the initial force that starts intentions; our intentions are nothing more than our creative desires. Creative power flows through us, as we become receptive to God's intentions. We then become connected to the pulsating force of God's Dabhar the original creative designing force behind the Creation.

Original design is the beginning of the process of the Creation. The design has the wisdom of the Creator. When the Creator creates anything it will always have the wisdom within it that was in the original act of Creation. Little children seem to know this because they always have to take things apart in order to see what is making it operate. All images seem to be bursting with wisdom. We were born with wisdom because we are the created product of God. God's wisdom is in everything; as it is above so it is below. Memory is the deposit of things that God puts into our minds. We have a genetic pattern that always directs our path in life. This genetic pattern is nothing more than memory that God has placed in us. There is mind, before there is wisdom. This is Ultimate Reality.

Reality Is Just Beyond Us

Ultimate Reality is always just beyond us. We can touch Ultimate Reality whenever we stretch our mind. Our mind puts us in contact with Ultimate Reality. We need to trust the thinking that permanency is always behind the things we see. Things are always more apparent than real. In Creation, there is a reality of permanency. This is why we must persevere in all things that we are called to do in life. Victory is always just beyond the horizon. When you can see the goal in your mind, it is just within your reach. All we have to do is just reach out and touch it. Dissatisfaction with what is, keeps you looking for what ought to be. Trust your dissatisfaction. Dissatisfaction signals that you are not where you are supposed to be. When you feel dissatisfied, you are forced to look for satisfaction. It is in our search for satisfaction that keeps us moving toward that which will satisfy our needs. This is why we need to persevere in life. It is going to take you into unknown territory.

Unknown territory always frightens us. We just have a fear of the unknown. We have to first make our minds strong enough to wander into the unknown. This is why the hero in life is important. We have respect for the hero because the hero goes off into the unknown, the hero fights the dragon, the hero fights to return to the community to tell the rest of us how to fight, and the hero waits in isolation for the next adventure. Isolation is just as frightening for most of us as the unknown. We just like to have other people around. There is something about isolation that makes us need to be around other human beings. Security is the human need for most of us. While we are in the world, we are always looking for security. This is why it takes courage to follow a dream. We have to have the courage to follow a dream because the dream will often lead us into strange territory and force us to face truth.

Truth Convicts You

Truth convicts us in spite of our attempt to ignore it. When we see truth in any form, we are confronted by it in a way that we are unable to ignore it. We may try to deny it, but we have to deal with it in the end. Realize that possibility is the part of truth that you must always recognize. It is the opportunity to make the faithful act by trying something new. However, if you do not take the time to study the nature of the truth, then you will lose the opportunity to faithfully create. Belief is right in front of you. When you want something to happen, you first have to believe that it will happen. Notice that we used faith and creating interchangeably. What we want to know, in the meantime, is that creation is the product of truth. This is why conviction is always necessary for the act of creation. Where we put out total mind in the process, is also where we place our total energy to make something out of nothing. In the heart of Creation we are trusting in the Dabhar as the Scripture says, "The word that goes forth from my mouth does not return to me empty [Isaiah 55:11]."

Vocation is a force that both pulls and pushes us toward the object that God has called us to deal with in this life. The Word of God gives shape to our vocation. We have several callings that come together into the product that God wants to bring into the world. Your vocation is a part of the purpose that God has for you in the Creation. It is the same as the old Chinese proverb that talks about our participating in Creation. The proverb says, "Humanity participates by nature in all cosmic events, and is inwardly as well as outwardly interwoven with them." Here is a truth of divine purity. Purity is the real idea of God. God always brings purity out of impurity. The ongoing process of creation requires that there must be a distillation process to bring purity out of impurity. Faith is the distillery. Our calling is the force that puts both the desire we have, and the force we have to achieve the purpose that God has called us to complete. We can complete it, for God interweaves the purpose into a perfect event. Perfection is in our gut. Believe this in your heart. The gut is the heart. We cannot help but seek perfection. Perfection is part of God's nature in our hearts. Therefore, all things are moving toward perfection. The basic fact is, vocation is a force that initially draws us to the desire for perfection. It brings us to a positive assertion of faith. Moreover, this positive assertion makes the mind seek, that which we assert. It is the assertion that causes the mind to believe that there is something out there. Faith validates the assertion.

We can never know for sure anything about anything. We have to make an assertion, and then move toward that assertion in faith. This is how we know that we are traveling in the generative way. Insight also helps our assertion. What we see on the inside of our self raises the assertion in the first place. There is a reflective process in nature that helps us to talk and listen to matter, in a way that we learn that everything has life. This is how the creative process is possible, because everything has life. The life in everything, responds to the life in us. The senses work with the life in everything. We sense what is there and what could be there, with just a little effort. All of this helps us to know when we are traveling in the creative pathway on the Path of the Via Creativa. The Technique of Generation leads us on our mission of creative faith. Mission means that we are traveling to faithful creation. When we are on a mission, we are seeking something. This is why our creativity should be unique to our purpose in life. There is an underlying harmony to the mission we are on. Harmony makes itself felt in life in a way that we are reminded of our purpose. In fact it is the memory of the lost harmony that keeps us moving toward that unique place that is in our inner self. Belief that there is a paradise keeps us looking for that unique expression which reflects this uniqueness in our inner self. There is no other way that your creativity can be unique. Without this uniqueness, in our inner self, everything we produce will be just another copy of that which already exists. Your mission is to bring something unique into the world. Your purpose for coming into the world is unique. This uniqueness is possible by thought alone.

Thought is a magic wand. Faith is the courage to use thought. We have the power to think things into existence. When we use thought, in the right way, we will bring things into the world that will benefit humanity. When we use thought in a wrong way, we will bring things into the world that will harm humanity. Reflections on the nature of the inner thought will always be revealed to the human mind. When we see the reflection of inner thought, as a useful strategy, our hearts always leap for joy. The reason that it is important to use thought in the right way is that we always get what we expect. Substance always yields to thought, as we have seen in life, thought influences the inner substance of matter, which causes it to take on different forms of energy. Speech is also powerful in spirituality.

Word is power. Just one word has enough power to blow up the world or to make a new world because creativity always starts with our belief. It must be understood that our words contain our beliefs. This is why Jesus informed us that we will be judged on how we used our words. Additionally, process operates on belief. In fact, belief is the conveyor belt on which process takes place. What we believe in our inner self is what happens. Creativity operates along a process that works on the thoughts of our inner self. Productions of the many different things that result from our words can always be traced back to a belief. Whatever we see in the world, is the invention of the mind.

Everything in the beginning started in the Mind of God. We cannot operate outside of mind. Again, this is why creativity always starts with our belief. We always receive what we truly believe we will get.

Negativity in the true sense of the word means nothing. Negativity is nothing. We cannot speak negativity without saying such words as no, not, never, and other words such as these. Nothing is what we have left when we have negativity. This is how our language could actually be a barrier to our creativity. Doubt is equally as detrimental to our creativity. When we doubt that we can do something or think that something is impossible, then we have built a barrier to our creativity. Language is either positive or negative in its essence. This is because language does not happen in a vacuum. There has to be at least one other person present in order to communicate. You must work to develop a language that is creative and positive. In Chapter 11, you will learn how to use the tool of Perception with the technique of Generation on the Path of the Via Creativa.

Chapter 11

Learning to See Again

Daniel saw de stone, rolin', rolin',
Daniel saw de stone, cut out de
Mountain wid-out hands.

In this spiritual, "Daniel Saw De Stone," the enslaved singers called attention to Daniel's perception. Daniel's perception emanated out of who Daniel was on the inside. Your initial perception is always influenced by your self-images. We usually perceive according to what we are on the inside. When you perceive something, it must first pass through the filter of your mind. The filter is that part of the mind that lets the things we want to pass through to our quality world permeate so that we can make it part of our self. "Our quality world is the all we want world."[16] Perception then is the result of the things that we put into our quality world. We can safely say that we shape our perception by what we want. The things we want make us perceive the things we want. When we see something, which meets our needs, it is usually already a part of our perception. Moreover, we form relationships with more than just people. We form relationships with everything that comes into our quality world. We are as much the makers of relationships, as we are the makers of other things. Therefore, the starting point of perception is always your self-image. Perception according to the Word of God starts in the heart, "Keep thy heart with all diligence; for out of it are the issues of life [Proverbs 4:23]."

The heart is the very center of the soul. This center is where we contact God located in our inner self. We are the carriers of God's divinity. This divinity is in the very heart of our being. The "third eye" is a common expression of the ability to see from the inner self into the things of this world. It is an art that the spiritual masters had to learn before each could be considered a spiritual master. A spiritual master or artistic master is in touch with his or her sensibilities. Sensibility is the way we get in tune with the things around us in a way that we see things others without our sensibility cannot see. The eye of the soul can be located. It is in the innermost part of the soul. Remember this, wherever you are, there is the center of your universe. When we recognize this, we are able to locate the eye of the soul because we will be able to look through the eyes of God.

This central point of the universe must be located in our inner self in order for us to experience God's divinity in our hearts. Your divinity is the Divine Mind in the center of your being. God is not out there where we must bring God down from the sky. God is in the innermost part of our being. We become still in the silence. This is what the spiritual masters of the Middle Ages called "re-collection," what the Quakers called "centering down," and what the enslaved African Americans called "anchored in the Lord." When we center the self, or the self is anchored in the Lord, we can focus on the innermost part of our being. We open our self to the divinity that is already in our centermost part. This is how your centered self is opened to your divinity. God is always at the center of the universe and when we center our self in God, we open the self to our divinity. God is a unified being. This is what we mean by the oneness of God. This unified oneness is the only position God will ever occupy. The oneness of God helps us to center ourselves in God. In fact, God is the collective whole of everything. God is not in everything but, everything is in the presence of God. God controls everything. All we control is our choice.

You Have Control of Your Choices

Choice is all we can control in this world. We can control nothing but our choices. Thus we are bound by the choices we make. We bare the consequences of the choices we make. Our choices are the result of our behavior. We, also, behave according to the choices we make. Behavior is always the thinking, acting, feeling, and the physiology of our choices. This is why one's life is the play one writes by one's choices. There is always a script that we write when we choose things. Nothing makes us choose what we choose, it is our free choice. However, everything we choose, we choose because we are trying to meet our needs at the time of choice. Uniqueness in this sense means more than just a singular type. It means that our life is the play we are writing. Nobody else can live it but the one who writes it. Your life is uniquely your total choice. Nobody else can choose your life for you.

Openness is the avenue that leads to the guarding angel of our life. We each have a guarding angel. When we get in touch with the child in us we also get in touch with our guarding angel. We get in touch with the child in us, as we acknowledge our dependency on God. Helplessness is a characteristic of the child. There is no time when we are not helpless. The gift of God's grace keeps us from harm and danger. The helplessness of the child is the force that draws the guarding angel to our side. Trusting is the greatest characteristic of the child. We are still childlike when we trust the Creator to make our way safe. The trust of the child of God keeps the guarding angel always watching over the path that the child of God is traveling. This is how the child in us sees its guarding angel. When we are able to see our guarding angel, it is because we perceive it from the inner self. You must keep your perception in a childlike state.

Our interior path leads to the beyond. We can see the beyond not by looking up but by looking inside. Your interior is the way to divinity. We are more awake inside, than we are outside. We see more inside of the soul than we see from the outside. Purity is seen better when we look inside. The purity of your soul is better than the cluttered outside of your soul, where everything is blurred by lines that are broken by scattered light. Faith is the way we see beyond the immediate. However, faith does not work with half belief and half-truth. There must be a clear path to the beyond. You must understand that you look into the beyond when you look into the center of your being. What makes your perception of divinity bright is your inward look, before trying to see your outward look. You must accept this truth before you can perceive that which is beyond.

Accepting what you see in the beyond is the starting point for entering into this mystery. Entering into the mystery of the beyond on the Path of the Via Creativa is flowing into the unknown. The whole universe, after all, is out flowing from God and flowing back to God. This flow refers to the constant flow of mystery. Yielding to this flow of the universe is the way to learn more about the mystery of the Via Creativa. Mystery is not that about which we cannot know something, it is rather that about which we cannot know everything. This is why we must yield to the flow of the creative mystery. As we yield to the flow, we learn more about how to use the technique of Generation in this creative mystery of out flowing. Perception is the best tool to use in order to flow with the mystery. As we perceive the creative mystery, we quieten our mind and ride the crest of divinity. As we are riding the crest of divinity, we pass into different layers of the mystery of creation. We project the creative mystery in the world.

Our projection is what lets us see whatever we see in life. Remember, 'There is nothing out there that we have not put out there.' It is the projections of our own making. The projections, as we have seen, come from the interior of our being. We can see eternity in a second of time, if we see that we already have eternity inside of our souls. Again, there is more to the things we see, than what meets the eye. All we have to do is look from the inside of our being. Creation is the projection of God. God is seeing what is here. God is "Being" you. What is here is here because God is seeing it here. For God to see is for God to say. Saying and seeing is the way God keeps things where they are when they are there. We participate in the saying and seeing of God when we perceive what is there. Our faith is our artistic expression. Faith is, after all, calling things that are not as though they were. Faith is the eternity in the grain of sand.

There is a creative rhythm in the flow of creative mystery. Rhythm is a part of everything because everything has rhythm. Your rhythm is the motion of your thoughts. The rhythm of your thoughts makes the music of your soul. Others recognize you by your rhythm. Your rhythmic impulse is clocked by the number of beats of the electrical sparks between the nerve cells in your brain. They pass faster than lightening and they keep us happy or sad depending upon how they produce the chemicals in our brains, which regulate our emotions. Our center is always that place in our inner self that is at rest, but the concentric circles moving out from our center are always dancing around us. They are bands of energy that influence everything around us in a good or bad way. For this reason, we must return to our center in order to keep our perception in line with the ultimate perception of God. When we operate from our center, we are following the motions of our thoughts that flow from our divine center. Behold the light of the divine flashing in the interior of your soul. This is how we see the extraordinary.

When we look on the divine light in our soul, we see the extraordinary. Look at the amazing art of mastering the ability to control the mind. You can see the reflection of the truth always making light flash for an extraordinary sight of reality. You can see the extraordinary in the ordinary sight when you anchor in the Lord for a quiet center. Consider that you can see the life in everything, because life in everything makes contact with the life in you. There is only life, not different kinds of life. The same life that is in you is in everything else in nature. Nature is alive. Your African ancestors believed and acted according to the belief that nature is alive, before the Western man came. The Western man called this kind of thinking "animism" and condemned it as demonic. However, now since the earth has become so devastatingly polluted by the materialistic thinking of Western man, they are beginning to talk about the rebirth of nature. Splendor is the best way to describe the extraordinary life that is in everything. Life is always in plain sight of the spiritual eye. We must, therefore, train our eyes to see the extraordinary in everything.

As we have pointed out earlier, beat is the measurement of the pulsating life in everything. We can hear the drums in the air that were beating long before we came upon the scene. It should always be possible to hear the drums beating in the air. Wind carries the sounds of the drums that were beating when our ancestors were trying to talk to each other. The wind is the matrix in which the whole universe is floating. The wind carries the voice of God in drumbeats and melodies that can be heard, when we are in tune with the universal music. Being receptive to the sounds enable us to hear the crying souls that have been trapped in the thick darkness of ages past. When we can hear the souls crying in the darkness, then we are listening to the drumbeats of the universe in the air. Receptive minds and hearts always commune with the rhythm of the Divine Mind. This is the very meaning of perception. Like the sensitive receiver of the radio, we can hear what others cannot hear, when we are in tune with the divine music. To have the music of the Divine Mind is the reason that we entered into the Incarnation Centered Spirituality, in the first place. This journey is substantially a journey into perception.

The five senses are for the perception of the universe. Irregular sounds can be noise to the untrained ear. However, when irregular sounds are perceived in the soul they become regular sounds of the soul. The soul acts as a sensitizer. We are the main objects in the universe; all other beings are conditioned by what we are. Noise is always sounds becoming music for the anchored soul. The ability to select is a trait of the soul that makes all things what they become. Things become what they are according to the selective ability of your soul. Each soul has to develop to the extent that it selects the things that make sense to it. Souls in tune with the universe can hear music in the noise around it. Even noise becomes music to the soul that is in tune with the celestial music filling the universe. This is also true of light.

Light is the glow of the darkness that every soul can watch. Watching the glow of the darkness is looking at the luminous darkness. Darkness lights up in the soul of the spiritual masters. Darkness is also inner light. This inner light helps us to see the luminous darkness. We can only see the darkness because it is light. The juxtaposition of light and dark enables you to see better. When we stop to think about it, we see that there is only light. What makes the difference is the degree to which the darkness is illuminated. In other words, the darkness is only apparent because the light is real. Intense light is hard to look at. Therefore, we need some darkness in order to be able to see. The intensity of darkness makes light visible. This is why light is not consumed by the darkness. Watching the glow of darkness is watching the darkness of glow. Darkness is never without some light. Walking in the light as God is in the light protects us from our own darkness.

Walking in the light is worship just as presence with God is worship. We are worshipping when we are in the presence of God without any false thoughts in our inner self. The presence of God is the presence of the worshiper. God is inside of us, therefore, we are standing in the presence of God anywhere we might be. Therefore, standing in the presence of God is also Holy Ground.

Holy is the state of being set aside for God's purpose in a state of wholeness. Anytime we are in the holy presence of God, we are in a state of wholeness. To be holy is to be whole! Insight is the product of being in the presence of God. This is why making worship a way of life is important to perception. The more we are in the presence of God, the better is our insight. The better our insight the better is our perception. Masters of the Spirit are always following the intention of God. Those who follow the intentions of God must always strive to follow the path that leads to mastering the spiritual life. This is why Incarnation Centered Spirituality is the path to wholeness. Harmony is the goal of preception.

There is in each person the memory of a lost harmony that nags us until we start seeking it. When we start seeking the lost harmony of our memory, we are following the intentions of God. It is God's intention that there will be a restoration of the harmony of the original paradise. Desire is shaped by the intention of God before it becomes corrupted by the desires of the flesh. The journey of every spiritual master is back to the intentions of God, which first begins, in the inner self. In Chapter 12, you will learn to deal with the artist in you, which is the intention of God.

Chapter 12

Rediscovering the Artist in You

'Zekiel saw de wheel, 'way up in de middle of de air,
'Zekiel saw de wheel, 'way in de middle of de air.
De big wheel run by faith, Little wheel run by de grace
of God; wheel wid-in a wheel 'way in de middle of de air.

Art is a sense of beauty that gives shape to the soul. The enslaved singers of the above Negro spiritual, "'Zekiel Saw De Wheel," understood the power of artistic imagination. We should have a sense of beauty that shapes our imagination as well. When we think of that which is beautiful, we are thinking of that which is true; truth is ultimate reality. When we encounter truth, we are in contact with the Ultimate Reality. Form must conform to truth because form is also the shape of our being. The spiritual master is aware of this. We have a spiritual form that is just as real as our physical form. Form is important when we are trying to understand Art. We must start with form, if we are to understand purpose. The function of anything is in its form. An object must be fit for the job if it is to be functional. It is always necessary to have a sense of beauty that shapes our being, if for no other reason, than to understand its function. In Christian Spirituality, there is never a sense of art for art's sake. Art and the artist are always functional in Christian Spirituality. Wonder is always the first thing we have, when we see truth and beauty functioning together. We see that there is a perfect harmony of all of the parts. Wonder is what keeps us in contact with the ultimate truth behind everything.

Dissatisfaction is the pain of the violation of our love of truth and beauty. The love of truth and beauty is always directing us in life by our emotion. Dissatisfaction is the only way that we express our feelings about falsity. Perfection is our inner need of the divine. We sense perfection in our soul. Because God created us to desire perfection, we are never pleased when something is imperfect. Completeness is the ultimate goal of our soul. We must experience completeness in everything or we will feel the pain of disharmony.

The love of truth and beauty will never let us settle for less. God created us to seek the fullness of the Creation. When the Creation around us is out of balance, we also are out of balance. The inner need for truth and beauty is a very strong impulse in our lives. We do not realize that we need truth and beauty for our souls, as much as we need food for our bodies, until we start to feel the sickness of undernourishment in our soul.

Learned sensitivity is part of human development. We are learners. We are continuously learning. When it comes to learning, it is harder to unlearn something, than to learn something. When we learn something, it becomes part of our being. We define our identity by what we learn. As we grow in life, we also develop. Keep in mind that when growth only means getting bigger, it is limited to the physical. In the spiritual sense, getting bigger is not getting better. What the world provides is a school in which we can grow and develop. Too often, we do more growing than we do developing in the schools of the world. Our greatest problem is what the schools are teaching. Education directs the teaching more to the material than the spiritual, more to our outsight, than to our insight. Insight is as much a learned process as anything else. We have the insight of that which is traditional and cultural. This insight is earthbound, but there is the insight of the spiritual. This insight is divine. We have to distinguish between spiritual and worldly insight. Spiritual insight is as much an act of unlearning as it is learning. We have to master a spiritual discipline in order to develop this insight of the Spirit. It is the necessity to commune with the divine that makes us develop a program of spiritual discipline to help us develop our insight. This is why acquired sensitivity is necessary for our journey. We have to work at it just like all other artists.

Images of divinity are real. We must learn the images of divinity if we are to become the spiritual masters that we need to be. When we understand the symbols of divinity we are able to express them just like any other artist. We are, after all, artists of the Spirit. Sounds are just as important as any other image. Sounds are audible images. They are the images of the divine. They are just as all other images—expressions of the divine presence of the Creator. Silence is also a symbol of divinity. You see divine images are as real as musical chords, colors and shapes. Understanding the symbols of divinity is important because once we learn the symbols of divinity, we are able to communicate, to humanity, the fine spiritual things of life just like any other artist. We are artists! Our medium is the Spirit. We work with the Spirit to bring forth treasures from the Divine Mind to our inner self. We have learned to communicate with our inner self in order to bring forth the divine thing into the world for humanity. These divine things are your core values.

Core values determine attitude. We are the expression of our core values.

We always take on the attitude of what is important to us. We have a value system that we are always trying to protect. Concentric circles flow from our inner core. The circles influence everything they meet as they spread out. It is possible for others to feel your attitude in the circles. This is why your attitude is important. It is your attitude that people sense and feel when they meet you. Transcendence over your attitude is very important because you cannot see your attitude until you rise above it. It is when we look at our attitude from a higher place, than from just face-to-face, that we will see our self the way other people see us. Again, we must rise above our ordinary self to see our attitude. Everything depends on our attitude because every person we meet will have an attitude. In fact our attitudes are the masterpieces we create.

Soul is the masterpiece that we have created as we traveled through time. We are the sum total of all that we have learned and have let come into our minds. Remember that we do have a quality oriented world. This is *the all we want* world. It is in this quality world, that we let all that we want enter. This quality world is what makes our soul what it is. We determine meaning for life mostly, by what we want. We are always trying to get what we want. What we want, makes us who we are at the time we are trying to get what we want. Reality for us is what we see in front of us. What we see in front of us is what we want. This is why we must be aware of what we want. You must control what you let come into your quality world. You must always be willing to sacrifice all for the masterpiece of your soul. This masterpiece is your creation; it is *the you* that you create from your conscious selection. This is your resurrection from spiritual death. You are letting your false self die so your true self can live in this physical world.

Resurrection is only possible after death. Death is necessary for the resurrection process to take place. This is why we must let some things inside die. Values are not always good. Some values should be discarded in order for us to get new values that will help us to get to where we want to be. The most important thing is for us to constantly look at our values. Non-responsiveness to things that we need to confront in us is the sure way of living with things that we should let die. It is not until we let things die in us, that we can experience the resurrection of new life. We must be aware that death does not mean that we no longer exist. It is therefore necessary that we do not hold onto things that we need to let go of. This is why in part you must experience the hero's death.

You Must be the Hero

To be heroic means more than bravery. Hero means the one who goes on a venture unwillingly. The hero starts out on a venture unsure of where it will lead. The hero is the artist seeking the dragon in the land that is threatening the people in the community. The hero finds the dragon, slays it, and returns home. It is as hard to return home, as it was to travel away from home, on the venture. The production of your masterpiece is your work of bringing something into the world that was not here before. This is the artistic way. The artist is the hero who goes on the venture to slay the dragon and comes back with a new way of seeing. The hero teaches the community this new way of seeing for its benefit. Exploration of the far country may take a long time; however, this exploration is very necessary. If you do not make the venture of the exploration into the far country, then there is no help for the community. The spiritual master is the hero who, goes to the inner self, explores what is there, and returns with a new way of seeing. This is why a return in resurrection power is the sense of art in spirituality. Discipline unequivocally is necessary!

You must give personal attention to the characteristics of the inner discipline of spiritual masters. The spiritual master is, after all, an artist. The heart of the artist makes the spiritual master want to reproduce the life of the Spirit in the world. Expression of the soul is the work of all artists. The spiritual master wants to tell the world about his or her experience with the Divine that is possible for all who want to find wholeness for their lives. Longing to tell the world about the divine in the innermost being is what makes the spiritual master develop the artistic skills in the first place. Jesus was the Master Spiritual Artist. When we watch his growth and development, we begin to understand His journey of the Spirit. We learn that there must be an inner discipline in our work of art because it is an expression of our innermost being. Spiritual discipline demands the divestment of self-interest.

Divested interest is the first rule of the spiritual life. This is when we do what needs to be done, and not because we want to take ownership. We can never own the Spirit. The art of the spiritual master is the development of the soul. The soul can never belong to the individual. All souls belong to the Creator. God is the rightful owner of the soul. Selfishness is the work of the enemy of creativity. When you become so self-centered, until you lose sight of the fact, that you can never own your creations, then you have lost the artistic sense of the Divine. Art is the expression of the soul for the benefit of humanity. When you are this kind of spiritual artist, you are the powerful soul influencing all other souls to seek the wholeness that you have found on your journey. Your journey into Incarnation Centered Spirituality in the path to wholeness is for your community. This demonstrates why all achievements must be disinterested products for the community. We do not own our creations; they become the property of the community, if they are of any material value.

Watch Your Material

Material is as much part of the artistic product as the form. In fact, the characteristics of the material, is what determines the form. We can never do more than the material will permit. This is the genius of art. Making the material do exactly what the material ought to do is the work of the artist. This is why knowing the material of creation is just as important as knowing the design of creation. We make creative contact according to the material we use. A certain touch is required with certain kinds of material. The material must conform to the design that the artist has in mind. Keep in mind, that form is a very important part of the artistic production. When the material meshes with the artistic design, it is almost completed. What is important, at this point, is the skill it takes to bring the material into the form. You can see why it is important to understand the material with which you are working. In Spirituality, the material is you. You are your initial work of art.

A work of art always begins with the idea of a design. The initial idea may be no more than a dot. Nevertheless, that dot grows according to the design that is in the mind of the artist. This is why the initial concept has to be there in some form before the artist can begin the work. In spirituality, the idea is in the innermost part of the self. It is the divine spark put there by God. It is this divine spark that is the image of God. In the creation of man, God left His divine image. It was placed there as part of God's purpose in Creation. Intention is the greatest expression of God. It is the force behind all of Creation. It is that intention that we keep encountering. When we encounter the intention of God, we are usually inspired to participate in the ongoing creation. All art is the participation in the ongoing creation. Intention is a force we have to deal with in life. It can be demanding. Outworking of anything is the expressed intention of that which is in the inside. The outworking of the Spirit is the spirituality of a person. It is the outworking of the "in working" of God's accepted intention for the person. We must accept God's intention before we can begin our work of spiritual art. It is necessary to perceive the design of the product before the work on the product begins. We choose the tools.

Use the Correct Tool

Tools are essential for the work at hand. The tools must be the right tools in order for the work to go well. Too many times, we try to do a job with the wrong tools. Successful production is the result of using the right tools. When the tools we need for the job are not available, then we design and make the right tools. It is highly essential that we consider the tools before beginning the work. The tools in spiritual work are just as essential. We must know what tools we will need before we begin our spiritual journey. Product is a process that yielded to a set of tools. We can just about know what tools were necessary by looking at the product. The process was, after all, the manipulation of tools on a medium. We should always get the right tools for the work we are attempting to do.

Understanding the parts of the whole helps us to have a clear perspective about the work. When we have a clear perspective of the whole, we will have a clear product. It is the understanding of the total process that produces the best product. In the spiritual journey, it is essential that we have a clear perspective of the journey. In Incarnation Centered Spirituality along the five-fold path to wholeness, it is essential that we start by embracing the Incarnation. If this is not done, the journey will be unclear. Wholeness will also be unclear. Purpose is the intention of God. Purpose is also the important tools in any work of art. Purpose is a tool. It is the best tool for working on the inside.

Design also reflects the purpose that is used to produce a work of art. All works of art must have a design because it is design that people see when they look at a work of art. A clear perspective is seen right away when we look at a work of art. The reason the artist needs a clear perspective is because it is the perspective that the artist is producing.

Art is an expression of an image that is in the mind of the artist. It is the creative work of one who is trying to deliver just what is seen in the inner self. The spiritual master has an image in his or her mind that he or she is trying to deliver to the world. Image is the most important thing about the spiritual journey. An exact copy is what the representational artist is trying to produce. It is very important that the copy match the image in the mind of the spiritual master. If this is not done then the spiritual master has missed his or her purpose. Nothing is worse than missing the image in the mind. This is why the spiritual master disciplines his or her life around a spiritual concept. Every spiritual master has a definite spiritual concept in his or her mind. It is this concept that the spiritual master has integrated into his or her life. Process works even when we are not aware of it. Process is the orderly movement of material into the right combination until the end results look like the concept. But in fact, the process is the least noticed but the most important. In Chapter 13, you will learn how to walk the Path of the Via Transformativa, using the technique of Life, with the tool of Transformation.

PATH IV

VIA TRANSFORMATIVA, LIVING FOR FREEDOM, JUSTICE, AND IDENTITY

Chapter 13

It's Time for Your Transformation

Lord I want to be a Christian in-a my Heart,
In-a my heart, Lord I want to be a Christian in-a
My heart. I just want to be like Jesus in-a my
Heart, in-a my heart. I just want to be like Jesus
In-a my heart.

The enslaved singer of this spiritual, "Lord I want to Be a Christian In My Heart," understood that it was time for their transformation if they were to move toward freedom, justice, and identity. The Path of the Via Transformativa is the result of struggling for freedom, justice, and identity in society and in history. It is soul renewal. The Path of the Via Transformativa, using the technique of Life, with the tool of Transformation will help you to become more like Jesus in your heart. Renewal is the first step in transformation. Your transformation is the result of the renewal that your soul has undergone. When your soul is renewed, then it is ready to move toward an entirely new orientation. Insight is the first thing that becomes new in the renewal process. We can see in a deeper way than we could see before. It then becomes apparent that we see better inside of us before we can see plainly, what is on the outside. It is actually that we see through our self-consciousness. It is our sense of self that we must become aware of before we can see further. Breakthrough is what we call this new way of seeing. It has to be a breakthrough because until the self moves toward the force of the renewal, there can be no enhanced way of seeing on the spiritual plane. Our insight is never any deeper than our ability to see inside of our self. This is really, why inner illumination is the first breakthrough to seeing clearly. The breakthrough opens our mind to new information and a new intuition. We become sensitive to new vibrations in our environment.

Openness is the necessary position of your mind, if you are going to be able to experience a transformed mind. The mind is what really has to be renewed with new information. The mind can become a powerful force in your path to wholeness. Seekers after wholeness in life, always start their seeking process with a transformed mind. They know that the mind is the most powerful part of a person. We are never able to rise above our mind. The mind makes us what we are. Change is the necessary process in the whole work of spirituality. Christian Spirituality is all about change.

It was Jesus who brought the possibility of human change into the world, in the first place, it is his spirituality that enables us to become agents of change. Change is the path to a transformed mind. Moreover, transformation must always be about your change of mind. A renewed mind increases your ability to give information a deeper meaning.

Meaning is a Growing Experience

Meaning is an experience that comes with a clearer vision of divinity. A clear vision of divinity precedes transformation because meaning is also a part of transformation. The average mind fails to recognize that meaning is something that we must grow into. We give a thing, or anything as far as that goes, meaning according to the level of our understanding. Meaning changes as we grow. The spirituality of the person grows from the point of understanding. We are always seeking understanding, even if we are unaware of it. Consciousness is more than just being alert. It is the position of understanding. There is always more to the reality of a thing than what we understand. It is your consciousness that makes you more than lower animals. We are forever expanding our consciousness. The expanded consciousness is transformation. Existence, in fact, is movement toward divinity. It is not blasphemy to desire divinity. It is, after all, the responsibility of each person to seek divinity. Existence is nothing more than participating in the divine being. The ultimate being is existence. There is no existence apart from the divine being. The process of transformation is the movement toward divinity. God is forever working on us to shape us into the image of His Son. Even after we die, this process of transformation is still taking place in our lives. Your brain controls everything about your physical life. The brain is the center of your experiences. It translates everything that your sense organs send to it. Your brain is also your information center. All of our experiences pass through the brain. The brain makes it possible for us to have a heightened awareness. This is why death is defined by the brain. When the brain is dead, even though the heart is still beating, death is declared. Sense transformation is a process that continues on after death. The brain makes us aware of the environment. This is why a heightened awareness makes transformation real. This is true because transformation continues on after death. Keep in mind that transformation is a vital process. Never stop growing intellectually! This is your ultimate act of faith. Fidelity is your ability to remain true to the heightened awareness that you acquire in life. We are responsible for living up to the knowledge that we have. We are only required to do that which we can do. Life is a strict judge. It always gives us just what we bargain for. It is after all our own contract with life that we are held responsible for in the end. We do make the choices in life that we are held accountable for in the end. I have said "in the end for a reason." It is because it is important that we realize that there is always an end where we are called to give an account of our living. Universe means that there is no hiding place in life. This is because there is a process in the universe that is always seeking to keep things as a unified oneness. There is no getting outside of the universe. Universe means that there is a cycling process that keeps taking all of the stuff in this world and reducing it into the universe that is always oneness, a unified whole. This is why a heightened awareness makes transformation real. We are always being brought back into the oneness of universe. As we undergo transformation, we become more in tune with the universe. The five-fold path of Incarnation Centered Spirituality leads to our transformation simply because our heightened awareness is the purpose of the journey. The utmost growth of transformation is compassion.

Compassion is the basis of transformation. The foundation upon which your transformation stands is compassion. Without compassion there is no Christian Spirituality. Spirituality is compassion of the soul flowing from God. Your life reveals the compassion of God. This is true of every person who would be a spiritual master in Christian Spirituality. Contemplation is a prayer life of the compassion of God. It is a fixed mindset on the goodness of God. When your mind is constantly thinking about the compassion of God, with the desire to reveal that compassion to the world, contemplation is more that just a shallow way of thinking. Emotions are stronger than logic. In fact, emotions are irrational. This is why we are to be in control of our emotions. When we realize it, we soon learn that emotions are what Satan deals with, when he wants to stop our progress in the Spirit. I mention this because you must not confuse compassion for simple emotions. To protect ourselves from Satan requires control of our emotions. The best way to do this is to act out of the love of God. Acting out of the love of God is an act shaped by your transformation toward wholeness, with the help of the Holy Spirit.

The Harmonious Relationship

Spirituality demands wholeness. Wholeness is the only way that your soul can live a life free of wasted energy. Spirituality is in fact nothing more than the acting out of the Spirit. The Spirit is not a passive entity just sleeping inside of us. The Holy Spirit is an active personal force trying to express Himself in our lives. Sexuality is important for the person who would be whole. This is because sexuality is also trying to be expressed. When there is a conflict with sexuality, then there is a problem with wholeness. We are always operating out of spirituality, personality, and sexuality. In addition, there is a very important part of transformation that must be in harmony with spirituality, personality, and sexuality. Personality is the great link between spirituality and sexuality. When this relationship is out of harmony then the total person is out of harmony. This is what it means to be a transformed person. When the total person is in harmony with the self, then the total person is transformed into a whole person. We confess our transformation to God.

Confession is a ready tongue to praise God in the act of transformation. The transformed person is always ready to confess to God. In fact, confession is a constant part of staying in contact with God. The confession is the act of emptying the soul of all impurities. Prayer always comes from a ready tongue. The prayer of the faithful makes the reality of God more useful. It is really an exercise of the Spirit in our own lives that prayer is designed to do. Prayer does not bring God down to us, but prayer brings us up to God. Prayer makes us aware of the God within the innermost part of our being. When we are praying, we are communing with the God inside of us. We have a straight path to God that leads into the center of our being. Now we will move from a discussion of prayer to a discussion of worship. Worship is a transforming act.

Worship is the practice of bringing our self into the presence of God by opening our self to God without trying to make God like us but by letting God see us for who we are. Worship is an honest approach to God. When God is before us in our self that is opened to God, then we are worshiping God. Worship does not mean ritual, but rather worship means presence. When we are present with God then we are worshiping God. This is what it means to have a ready tongue to praise God in transformation. Transformation is an act of praise and worship that meets our needs.

Needs serve as an incentive to control behavior, so that you can achieve things in life, which are essential to our becoming a whole person and who we are supposed to become in life. Keep in mind that you have the ability to control your behavior from your inner self, just because of what you need in life. Your needs are the reason you do whatever you do. Keep in mind that your behavior is designed to meet your needs. We are always behaving. We behave because we must behave. The human is a behaving organism. We must behave. Choice is what we use to meet our needs. We don't always make the right choices, but we are constantly making choices. There is no way we can avoid making choices. Human behavior is made up of the four elements of thinking, acting, feeling, and physiology. Behavior is total. It is always these four elements in every behavior. This is why we can control our behavior from the inside. Nothing on the outside of us can make us behave. We have long thought that we are conditioned to behave. Now, while this is true with lower animals, it is not true with human beings. Human beings have the ability to make choices based upon rational thought. Because we do have the four elements of total behavior, we can control our behavior from the inside rather than the outside. This is why our transformation is always returning us to the mind of simplicity. The more complex our lives become, the more we need to practice simplicity.

Simplicity is the desired state of mind. When we are operating with simplicity, we are operating with a single heart. The single heart keeps us in contact with God. Transformation is possible because we are capable of having a single heart. When we think of the heart in spirituality, we are thinking of the inner centermost part of our being. The single heart is one that is in a state of simplicity. Focus is not possible if there is no single heart. It is necessary to keep the focus on the single purpose that is pulling and pushing us towards our objective. We are, after all, on a journey to wholeness. This journey is a path along the Via Transformativa with the technique of Life. This having been said, we must keep our mind on the path. A single heart is necessary for dedication. If there is no dedication to do what we are doing, then, we will have a double mind. A double mind is incapable of focusing on a single thing. The mind wonders and makes conflicting decisions when it is in a state of double mindedness. Dedication is necessary when we are journeying toward transformation. Dedication to the act of repentance is the single act of transformation. The mind is always in a constant state of renewal through repentance for the sake of our transformation. Repentance is renewal.

Renewal is a sense of liberation. It is the promise of a freedom from our mental chains and our spiritual burdens of captivity. Captivity is the single most troubling problem of transformation because it is an act of conforming to this world. When we are in a frozen state of mind and soul, we are completely unable to move to the place where we must go through our transformation. Renewal of the mind helps us to find that place in life that leads to our transformation. Transformation is after all the changing into another form. The form that we are changing into is the form of a free being, one who realizes that the soul is free to be what it should be. It is the freedom to be that helps us to become a changed person. The freedom from that, which holds us captive, is the freedom of being that, which we are destined to become. Thinking, as we have seen, is the means to our liberation. What we think has more control over us than anything else we can imagine. It is our thoughts that keep us captive or that liberate. When we change our thoughts, we change our feelings. Thinking to the soul is what poison is to the body. Poison can be medicine for the body or it can be toxic to the body. It depends on how we use the poison. Thinking is like that; it can make us well or it can make us sick. Spirit is the power that holds it all together. The spirit never gets sick. We are not trying to make our spirit free. The spirit does not need to be liberated. This is why we do not need a sense of a liberated spirit. We already have a liberated spirit. It is our soul that is held captive and that is in need of liberation. Having discussed renewal, liberation of the soul, and spiritual freedom, we can now move to redemption as an act of deliverance.

Redemption is a total experience. It is the experience of being liberated from the market of the flesh. You are held captive in your flesh by the condition of your soul. The flesh that cries out for freedom; this is important to know because most of us think that it is our spirit that needs to be liberated. Jesus came to the world to buy us back from the slave market. Redemption is the beginning of the New Life that is set free in the flesh. Human nature does not know the Spirit since the Fall of Man. The Spirit was made to wait for the liberation of the flesh in order to act as a living force. This is the function of our tripartite being of spirit, soul and body.

When the natural man is set free then the Spirit can reunite with the body as a living force in a way that there is harmony between the Spirit and the flesh, this includes the soul. The soul after all is the fleshly part of the self. Beyond the power of the flesh, is the anointed power of God that makes us alive to God. Beyond is more of a process than a place. When we learn that the things we spend most of our time trying to accomplish are what the Bible call vanity of vanity, then we will become aware of the value of living beyond the flesh with anointed power of the Spirit.

Consecrated spiritual power in the life of the believer is the beginning of the anointing power that Jesus came into the world to give us. We are desperately in need of the consecrated power released through resurrection of Jesus that came in the person of the Holy Spirit. This is why the calling of Jesus is more than an act of making us a part of the work of Jesus; it is the total involvement in the new life that Jesus brought into the world. It is the reason why our transformation is possible. We must have a sense of the calling of Jesus on our lives before we can ever become a part of the new life in Jesus Christ. Jesus is about the new life. In addition, the new life is not imparted to us until we sense a calling from Jesus. This is important because if we were just able to take up this new life on our own power, then Jesus would not have needed to come into the world. The ways of God are hard to know until you become part of the new life. We refer to his new life as the New Birth. The New Birth is a new supernatural life released in our natural life that elevates us above ordinarily natural people, to appear before humanity.

Appearance is the only way others can see us. It is for others that we are made to appear in the way in which we appear. Others must see the image of what we are appearing to be as spiritual masters. There should be a Christ image that is seen by the outside world. Dependence upon this image is what makes the world aware of your new life in Christ. If the world cannot see the image of Christ in you, then Christian Spirituality would be just another philosophy of religion. The ability to depend on the Christ image is necessary for both the image bearer and the persons looking upon the image. Sacrificial living as the transforming power of the Spirit is the first way the image is manifested to others. The life put on the blocks for the good of others is both rewarded and revealed to the world. There is no genuine life in Christ, if there is no image of Christ that others can view in our lives.

Real divinity is embraceable. Embracing divinity is the first act of those, who would seek to follow the Path of the Via Transformativa, to wholeness. We are broken people in our natural life. The supernatural power released by Jesus, must make us whole. Embracing divinity is the only objective way for those who seek wholeness. Divinity is the reality behind Creation. Divinity is the divine presence in Creation that gives it shape and substance. This divinity is what we call Ultimate Reality. Ultimate Reality is more of an inside experience than an outside experience. There are those who try to explain the Ultimate Reality, by trying to reference some point in the world. However, the Ultimate Reality must be an inside reality before it can be an outside reality for us. The truth of the matter is that God is and has always been in us. Treasure is a personal possession of valuable resources. This is true in the spiritual more than in the natural. The saying that one man's treasure is another man's trash is very true in the spiritual life. The spiritual life is personal and private. Trying to tell somebody else about the spiritual life is like trying to describe the sunset to a person blind from birth; it takes the act of conversion.

Conversion is the act of becoming a witness to the divinity in the world. God converts us to converse with others, about the supernatural life in Jesus. When we converse with others about the purpose of God, we have to do more demonstrating than demanding. This is why becoming a witness to the purpose of God is formed inside of believers, by the transforming power of God. Believers cannot form the witness in themselves. Witness means that we have firsthand knowledge of an experience. We can describe it to the best of our ability, but as we have seen, it cannot be done well. There are some things that we just do not have words to describe. Fortunately, everyone can see behavior. When the behavior looks like it has a spiritual element, then we are able to talk about that element. When supernatural power becomes our means of operating in this world, we will have help from on high. When something is extraordinary, we can see it. It attracts our attention. After this extraordinary experience, we have the witness formed inside of us. Then the conversation about the Word of God can begin about this extraordinary attraction. You have just finished using the tool of Transformation in the Path of the Via Transformativa with the technique of Life. In Chapter 14, you will learn about putting your life in the context of the divine unity of the Creator. This Chapter will help you put your life into the context of living in the unity of the divinity as a daily practice. You will learn how to use the tool of Living as Jesus, in the Path of the Via Transformativa, using the technique of Life.

Chapter 14

Putting Your Life in Context

Walk together children, don't you get weary,
Walk together children, don't you get weary,
Oh, talk together children, don't you get
weary, there's a great camp meeting in the
Promised Land.

This chapter is about life in the context of unity. This chapter focuses on putting your life in context. It is clear that the enslaved singers of this Negro spiritual, "Walk Together Children," understood the context of unity. They recognized that they had to walk together. Unity was important to these singers. They were right; unity is a participatory experience. The words of "Walk Together Children," reveal that the singers had sensed a relationship between walking together and the "camp meeting in the Promised Land." This is really the context of life. The metaphor of the camp meeting in the Promised Land alludes to the freedom, justice, and identity that motivated the singers. They never forgot this context of their existence. They meant a camp meeting in earth as well as in heaven. To these singers, Christianity was more than a pie in the sky. It was their practical way of living in order for them to stay whole in a broken society. Christian Spirituality is about spiritual union. The scripture says, "But he who is joined to the Lord is one spirit with Him [1Cor. 6:17]." Moreover, spiritual union is the main reason for spirituality in the African American experience. You must rediscover this context for your life. The enslaved creators of this spiritual understood that Jesus came into the world to help everyone participate in the unity of the Godhead. Unity is the position of the oneness of reality. It is a union of vitality. The Ultimate Reality is the sense of the unity of all things. In other words, the Ultimate Reality is when you experience the unity of all things, which is the knowledge that what we experience in our daily lives is nothing but the construction of our culture. Beyond the construction of our culture is the direct experience of the presence of God, which is wholeness. This Technique of life is the context that leads to the experience of unity. We must participate in this unity if we want wholeness in a broken world. Wholeness is the participation of the many in the one. If we are whole, we are in harmony with the oneness of the universe. The wholeness of the personality is the harmony of the personality, the sexuality, and the spirituality. Moreover, divinity is the experience of unity. When we are in unity with the universe we are also in unity with the divinity of the universe. There is no greater hand behind the universe than the unity of the Creator. The Creator is the total Godhead. Moreover, where the Godhead is, there is unity. We center the self when we are in the unity of the Godhead. The context of life is the center of divinity. Centering your life is putting your life in context.

Centering the Self in God

Centering is the state of being where the total self is in the center of the Godhead. You concentrate to bring self in accord with the Godhead. The concentration must be in unity with the Creator. Concentration is the ability to stay focused on a thing with the purpose of perceiving the total essence of the thing. There is the ability to think about a thing until we understand something about it. However, concentration means more than just understanding a thing. It means the perception of the total essence of the thing. The journey is a long concentrated effort to stay in the path that leads to the desired objective of wholeness. This is why you need to stay centered in your inner self in a broken world. Now listen carefully, seeking is staying in that which you are seeking. Seeking is more than just looking for something. Seeking is living with a purpose. Life is seeking.

Seekers are looking for the wholeness that comes with freedom, justice, and identity in the divinity of the universe. When we are looking for the ultimate reality in life, we start a seeking that becomes a journey toward wholeness, which is freedom, justice, and identity. When we stay on the path of the journey, until we are aware of the brokenness of the world, we become aware of our own brokenness. It is then that the desire for wholeness becomes the force of life. Options for becoming whole will appear. When we see the options for wholeness, then we become aware of the choices we have for becoming a whole person. The options hide from us until we become aware of our own brokenness. The gospel then becomes more than just a story about the incarnation of Jesus. There are many stories of the incarnation of gods. However, the gospel becomes a practical roadmap for those seeking wholeness in this broken world. It becomes the Word of God that leads to eternal life, which means in this case, the wholeness that is the gift of God. When we discover this truth, then we will have discovered the beginning of the reality of receiving wholeness as a personal message from God. You can now embrace the New Birth as your new beginning of divine life.

We experience unity in the rhythm of the supernatural activities in the New Birth that comes from God. The birth that comes through the Spirit is the life that flows from the rhythm of the Godhead. We are born of the Spirit for communicating the rhythmic flow of divinity. This flow is an eternal rhythm of divinity. Harmony is the natural experience of this flow. Harmony is in everything in the universe. There is nothing that is not seeking harmony in the universe. Logic is the best evidence of this harmonic flow. Things must make sense in life or there is no way of understanding anything that is in the universe. The logic in the universe is the evidence of the mind behind the Creation. There is a flow in Creation that passes through everything in an orderly, harmonic, and rhythmic way that makes it possible to track the logical existence of everything. Nature is alive.

New Birth and Innocence Recovered

Innocence is the qualification for seeing the aliveness of nature. When we are innocent of the evil of natural order, then we will begin to see the heartbeat of nature. The heartbeat of nature is the pulse of life that is nature. Life in anything can sense the life in everything. We learn from the Word of God that we are dead until we are alive in the New Birth. The life of Christ is the life of the seeker. The Scripture says, "You have died and your life is hidden with Christ in God [Colossians 3:3]." The New Birth is our recovery of innocence. It is with this recovery of innocence that we are able to see the aliveness of nature. We see it from God's point of view--we are sensitive. Sensitive is the ability to receive divine stimuli and to react to it. When we are unable to react to the experiences in life then we are unable to see the aliveness of nature. Spiritual relationships are built on the ability to see the aliveness in nature. When we are able to form relationships with nature, we are in a state of mind that enables us to sense the aliveness in all things. Life is Life. There is no other way to understand life than by recognizing that life itself is unique. Life cannot die. Life must be understood as a substance rather than as a quality. Eternal life is more than a quantity of time--it is a life of transcending ability. Life in the New Birth is reconciliation. Reconciliation is cooperation with Creation. When we are reconciled to the Creator then we are reconciled with the Creation. Our life in Creation is alienated from Creation when we are alienated from the Creator. You want to cooperate with Ultimate Reality in Creation. Then, realize that the things we call reality are under a law, which is the same below as it is above. Consider that peace is the right relationship between the Creator and the laws of creation. We are not able to sense the laws of creation until we are able to have a harmony with the laws of creation. A relationship is always about cooperation. If you want to have a relationship, then you must be willing to abide by the laws of relationship. Completeness comes from the harmony between Creator and Creation. It is this sense of completeness in Creation that makes us seek the ability to cooperate with the Creator.

The technique of Life is the pathway to satisfaction. Dissatisfaction in life is an indicator that something is wrong in life. We will always feel dissatisfied until we are made to feel complete. When we feel complete we will feel the satisfaction that we have reached the ultimate reality of unity. But until we feel complete, we will seek completeness. Awareness of the feeling of completeness keeps us seeking the Ultimate Reality of wholeness. When we are awake to life in the Creation, we are awake to the possibility of completeness. Restlessness is the way we live in a world of brokenness. Completeness is a component of wholeness. Wholeness is the human experience of divinity; however, in Incarnation Centered Spirituality, there is the ideal that there must be completeness in everything. This completeness in every object is the only satisfaction for man, made in God's image. We can find no peace after we have discovered the possibility of completeness. We will always feel compelled to keep moving toward God's ultimate reality of personal wholeness for us. The ideal of completeness is not only possible, but it is necessary in your life. It is necessary in order to produce disillusionment with the world that drives you to the spiritual life. Life calls to life and life answers. Life answers by seeking for wholeness in a broken world. This is a positive act of unifying, clarifying, and accomplishing in you, the same sort of summing up and reconciliation that was accomplished in Jesus. The scripture says of Jesus, "and by him to reconcile all things on earth or things in heaven, having made peace through the blood of His cross [Colossians 1: 20]." More precisely, Jesus introduced us to something more than religion. He gave us God. This is the spiritual meaning of that which is positive.

Positive is that which keeps us moving toward the yeses of life. The yeses of life keep us moving in the direction of personal wholeness. Negative is really the absence of positive. The positive in life protects us from that which is negative. Optimum is the best location between that which is negative and that which is positive. When we are traveling at the optimum speed, we are traveling at the best speed for the condition of the road. This is true of our journey in life; we must always seek the optimum speed to travel. Wholeness best describes that which the ultimate goal in life is, that which keeps us on the journey. Wholeness possesses the promise of restoration of the spiritual endowment made by God, dating back from the act of creation. It is the restored harmony of the memory of Eden.

Harmony is Unity of the Spirit

Harmony, as was pointed out above, is the result of oneness with Creation in believers. Harmony in believers helps them to walk in step with the Creator. Until harmony is restored, there can be no unity of Spirit with the Creator. Communication enables the believer to know what the Creator is saying both in scripture and in nature. There is no misunderstanding the Creator when there is a harmony of Spirit. The heart knows something the head could never understand. This is why faith is a matter of the heart. Now while it is true, that faith must first be belief in the intellect, before it can be a heart thing, nevertheless, it must ultimately become a heart thing, before it can be an authentic faith. Communication is the act of communing. When we understand, we will become better communicators. Understand that flow is the quality of created motion. All things flow out from God and back to God. Some people catch this flow and others miss it because they are not in communication with the Oneness of Creation. This is what a Oneness of Creation means to believers. Oneness also means that we are united in Spirit, soul, and body. The Oneness of Creation means that there is only one divine flow out from and back to God through believers. Believers know they are in the flow because they are in harmony with Creation. It is an ecological dance.

Ecology is the study of the harmonious relationship of the environmental condition. This sounds simplistic, but ecology is really much broader than that. Ecology is really the study of the harmony of Creation. This perspective justifies why there must be supernatural obedience to the Creator. The real truth is that there is no Creator who is not supernatural. But this is not the understanding shared by everyone. There are some who believe that Creation is eternal. In other words, matter itself is supernatural and therefore there is no need for a supernatural being. This idea is dispelled by the existence of laws. Creation cannot develop laws. For there to be laws, there must be a lawgiver. As we have said, the same law that governs nature is the same law that governs heaven. As it is above, so it is below. Law is more than something we develop to make things work. Law is something we discover that is already there and already making things work. Nature does not just run according to its own laws. Nature is the product of laws in action. There is, at the core of nature, an energy working according to laws. It causes things to come into being and to pass away.

Subatomic particles are changing into substance and energy operating within the laws of relationships, which get their force from the supernatural power that is still in the act of creating. You must have a supernatural obedience to environmental laws. This obedience is submission. Submission is putting yourself under the power of another. The submission of the believer, seeking unity in life, is the voluntary act of bowing to a higher power. This higher power is not an abstract power but a real concrete Creator. The Creator is concrete in the Son of God. The Son of God is also the Son of Man, which makes him not only the Savior but also the human example of submission. His example is how we learn the true meaning of submission. Jesus shows us how to submit to the Father as an act of total obedience. The believer leaves everything up to the Father. Enlightened souls always recognize what is agreeable for submission to the holy in life.

The enlightened soul must first be illuminated with the fire of divinity which comes as a potential reality with the New Birth. This fire is always smoldering deep in the core of the self. The fire was not extinguished with the fall of humanity. The Creator made us in His own image. And, that image cannot be extinguished. While it is true that the Image of God may never come to light in the individual, it is also true that the Image of God is always a potential in the individual. When the soul is enlightened by the illumination of the light of God, it is then, that it is pleasing for the submission to the holy in life. This pleasing time for submission is also the beginning of the journey of Incarnation Centered Spirituality. In the technique of Life, opportunity becomes more than just an empty word. In fact, the Word makes opportunity possible. Submission to the Holy in life is not an opportunity until the Word of God makes it possible in the believer's life. The Trinity is working in the technique of Life. The Trinity is always in the act of transforming you into the likeness of Jesus.

Trinity is more than the Father, Son, and Holy Spirit. It is the possibility for the personal connection of the Godhead in the life of the individual. Although the word Trinity was coined by a theologian in the fourth century, it is nevertheless an accurate expression of connection. The connection in the Godhead is the unity of personality for God and for you. The three in one is more than a spiritual ideal; it is the practical evidence of this unity in life. Unity in life is the possibility that lives in the Godhead. The Godhead cannot tolerate division in life. Division, as a matter of fact, is the original sin. When there was a separation in Creation of the unity that is necessary in Creation, the Godhead reacted with redemption. Jesus is the result of the reaction of the Godhead to the division in Creation. Division in the universe did not happen until man was separated from the Godhead. Because humanity is the original representative of God in Creation, Jesus is the present representative of God in Creation. Jesus became man in Creation so man could become divine in Creation. The Holy Spirit is to redemption what fire is to gold. When the Holy Spirit comes into the individual's life the purification process begins. This is a process that must be continued by the work of the individual. It is the faith of the individual that begins the process, but it is the work of the individual that continues the process. The work makes it possible for a personal connection with the Godhead in life. The good news is that there can be a personal connection with the Godhead in this life.

Faith is revealed in behavior. The behavior of an individual will always express the faith of the individual. In the biblical sense, faith is trust in God's way of salvation. When we substitute anything else for salvation in this life, it is not faith. Faith is neither luck, concept, nor coincidence. Many times we are talking about a concept, luck or coincidence when we think that we are talking about faith. Faith is always about Jesus because faith is rooted in Jesus' faith in God and our faith rooted in Jesus' faith. We participate in the faith of Jesus. Faith always imitates Jesus in this life. It is always a total dependence on the Father for everything in life. Nothing is left out of this dependence. If we depend on anything in life for anything in life, then it is not faith.

Hope is the unseen thing for which, we are trusting in God. We have a hope that gives shape to all the hope in our lives. It is the hope of glorification. Glorification makes it possible for hope in life. Glorification is only a part of salvation, but without glorification there is no salvation for the individual. The hope of the believer is comprehensive. It includes the entire condition for anticipating the things that pertain to faith. Love is also part of the believer's life that is expressed as the medium through which faith operates. The joy that is expressed in the life of the believer is the combination of faith, hope, and love. It is this combination that culminates in unity in the life of the seeker. However, it is discipline that makes spiritual maturity possible.

Spiritual maturity must be observed in the life of the individual or it is not spiritual maturity. Spiritual maturity is the part of personality that shows up in the total behavior of the individual. Sharing is the evident outcome of spiritual maturity. Sharing is an act that enfolds the situation with an aura of caring, which illuminates the situation with a divine light that is healing and helping. The recipients of the love of another person are both healed and helped. Sharing is only sharing when it is done in love. This is why spiritual maturity can be seen only in the whole person. The whole person is spiritually mature. Maturity is a position of perfection. This perfection is a state that is forever growing. It is always moving toward completeness. It is essential to understand that perfection is a declared state. It is a state of righteousness that is characterized by holiness. This is what makes the unity of the individual an operational quality that can be seen in the life and work of the believer. Holiness is the potential for wholeness. For this reason, the New Testament refers to the believers as saints.

Hidden joy is another quality that marks the believer who uses the technique of Life to wholeness. The most unifying characteristic of wholeness is hidden joy. This joy is hidden because it is not known to unbelievers. Unbelievers consider this joy an artificial type of positive thinking or some kind of behavior that is motivated by things in life. The hidden joy, however, is the ability to respond to the unity in life that is openly expressed. This expression is always in the form of joy. The inner self is sensitive to that which is divine when the spiritual fire has been ignited. The illuminated inner self is even able to see the glow of darkness. This glow of darkness draws the inner self toward the divine center where the core of divinity is located.

In the universe there is a movable center. Transformation is the changing of the individual from the person to the potential. We must remember that the presence of potential in the person makes personal transformation possible. Transformation can be understood as the act of transforming human nature. This act is a continuous process until human nature becomes the likeness and image of Jesus. Like Jesus, we find perfect unity with the Creator and the Creation when God restores His Image in us. Unity is the context of your life. This context is the total development of your personality. In Chapter 15, we will learn that personality is the outgrowth of consciousness. Personality development is on the Path of the Via Tranformativa, using the Technique of Life in the context of unity for letting yur true self out.

Chapter 15

Letting Your True Self Out

It's me, it's me, it's me, O Lord, An' I'm
standing in the need of prayer, O, Lord.
Tain't my mother or my father, but it's me
O, Lord Standin' in the need of prayer.

In the midst of all of the experiences that you have accumulated in your life there is a "me" inside of you trying to get out. You and you alone, must let your "me" out. Your "me" inside of you is your true self. Therefore, letting out your true self begins with your recognition of your inner "me." The enslaved singers of this Negro spiritual, *Standing in the Need of Prayer*, are very conscious of who is standing in the need of prayer. They sang, "It's me, it's me, it's me O Lord." They were letting their true selves out into the environment. Their "me," about which they sang, is their true personality. This is the result of their raised consciousness. It is necessary that your consciousness be raised to the level that you can recognize your "me" inside of you. Consciousness makes the difference in human beings. Moreover, the difference between each human being is the level of consciousness.

However, the whole Creation contains consciousness. The difference is the level of consciousness. Consciousness is higher in dogs than in rocks, but there is a level of consciousness, even in rocks. Even rocks have personalities. It is very important that you let your personality out. Be aware that personality in spirituality means your "me" inside of you, that you must develop, and let out into your environment. Personality, in this sense, is possible because of your consciousness. Your personality is the level of consciousness that you have developed. Your consciousness is the way you approach things in the world. Your consciousness enables you to respond to other things and other people in your world. Your uniqueness is the obvious thing that reflects your level of consciousness. Your uniqueness sets you apart from all other human beings. This is a logical manifestation of your real "me."

Logic is more than just the way we think. It is the machinery of your mind. This machinery makes it necessary for us to think in a logical way. It is always necessary for us to reason things out, because we are logical beings. Logical thinking is as much a part of your being as your eyes are for seeing. Moreover, Logos, by the way, is the way the Bible speaks about the reasoning mechanism in God and in human beings. Logos is the thinking part of the Divine Being who created the universe. The Logos, moreover, is that divine ability that holds Creation on course. This reasoning ability of the Creator also makes the human being a reasoning being. It is as necessary for human beings to reason as it is for human beings to sense that there is a power higher than human beings. It does not matter what this power is called, it is still recognized as the higher power. Emerging powers are nothing more than powers that are always with the Creator. It is just that the human has to develop consciousness to the extent, that the reasoning ability is able to comprehend, the phenomena always present. When we realize how long it took human beings to recognize the use of fire, and the wheel, then we will begin to see how long it takes human beings to develop rationally. Letting the true self out is the process of information. It is the information of your "me" waiting to get out.

Information is another way of saying development. Things are informed in us; it does not matter if it is an idea, or a liver. Everything is informed in the human being. When you are being informed you are growing in ways that you will let out. You can only let your potential out. Now, if the potential is not there, then there is nothing to be informed. However, be assured you have the potential to become your "me." Intellect is informed in human beings. The intellect is nothing more that accumulated experiences. This is what early educators called the apperceptive mass. This apperceptive mass is always in the state of informing. This is why identity of your "me" should be your first matter of business in your spiritual journey. United components of the personality depend on your ability to identify the parts. Your personality is closely related to your identity of your apperceptive mass. Who your "me" is depends mostly on, what the person experiences, and how the person is able to identify the experiences in life, this really is what, after all, shapes one's own life. This is why the identity of your "me" inside of you should be your first matter of business in personality development. Openness is the state of mind that perceives anything in your environment. Like a sponge sucking up water, your mind expands with experience. It never gets too full because it is constantly systematizing information in the categories where it belongs. This breaking down and building up of information is the method whereby the personality is developed in the environment where it is located. Hereditary endowment is not an isolated part of your personality. It is an integral part of your whole person. Hereditary endowment and environmental experience both work together to form personality. However, the personality likewise is the part that makes the individual unique. The uniqueness of the individual develops from within. Letting your true self out is about releasing your "me" which is your developed potential. Therefore, letting out your true self is the same as letting out your potential.

Potential is developmental ability. Each individual has potential to develop into what the individual is supposed to become in life. None of us just dropped into the world by accident. Each one of us comes into the world with a purpose. Your purpose is equipped with the potential to develop into the persons you are to become. Many things in life, such as accidents, lifestyles and such things as these affect potential. Nevertheless, the potential of intelligence stays opened to experiences the entire time the individual is in this world. Intellect is a potential that determines how much the individual is able to perceive in life. However, intellect is not a fixed thing but it is rather ever expanding. The intellect is the ability to know that one wants to know. This intellect is influence by desire to know. The desire to know automatically develops the intellect for knowing. When we really put our minds to something, we usually achieve it. Directed potential is the best way to describe what real intelligence is in the final analysis. The most important thing to keep in mind is that everybody has the intelligence to accomplish whatever his or her purpose is for coming into the world. The lives of certain people can demonstrate this fact. Einstein, for instance, had the potential for mathematics, George Washington Carver had the potential for botany, Alexander G. Bell had the potential for inventions, and Jesus had the potential for spirituality. It is about what you are in tune to that the potential is activated accordingly.

Being in tune is a way of saying you are in harmony with something. When you are in tune with a thing, you are able to communicate with it. Being in tune with a thing is also a function of personality development. This is why learning how to communicate makes a difference. The singers of the above spiritual were communicating with the Creator about their "me" standing in the need of prayer. Communication is much more than just talking to someone. It is really an act of being absorbed by someone. When something or someone absorbs us, we are in tune with it. You must understand that everything around you communicates with you. You also communicate through the way you walk as well as the way you talk. Your body communicates without even saying a word. The truth of the matter is we cannot help but to communicate. Personality is a communicator. Personality communicates the level of awareness. Awareness is consciousness at some level.

Awareness makes the individual a conscious communicator. This is what we must strive to become. If you want to express your "me" then you must become aware of what you are communicating. This is because there is no time that we are not communicating. We are not aware most of the time of the messages we are sending out. In the spiritual journey, and we are all on a spiritual journey, we must learn how to communicate the right message. The real fact of the matter is that we are in the world to communicate the one message that we came into the world to communicate. Human being means more than we are in the food chain at a level higher than other animals. To be human means that we are able to communicate with the Creator in a way that no other animal can. This is why history is so important to human beings. It is through history we learn our meaning and purpose in life. History is a storehouse of information that is vital to human welfare. This is the main reason why learning why communication makes the difference is necessary. You receive the just reward for knowledge of your history. This, in fact, even if you are not aware of it, is the demand on your life. This is how your "me" is released.

Rewards are desirable or undesirable outcomes of our actions. We like to receive positive rewards for what we do. In fact, the drive of the spiritual life is positive rewards. Reward is, in fact, what shapes our values. You must know, this is very important knowledge, that your value system is the collection of rewards. We must value the things that will make us feel whole. There is, however, a distortion of values in some of us. When values are distorted, they are bent out of the order they should be in. Truth, for example, should come before falsity in the order of values. Punishment is the usual reward for distorted values. Punishment is another way of saying there is a negative reward for the negative values. Most of us do not desire negative rewards for our actions. However, the truth of the matter is negative personalities receive negative rewards. They have been shaped by their value system in such ways that negative to them is positive. Although, choice is the real reason we receive our values. We choose the things we receive and the things we receive are the things we want, this includes both rewards and punishments. Therefore, we must be sure that we are developing a positive personality, that we are making a proper assessment of what we mean by positive and negative in life.

In regard to choice, you must be aware that the ultimate position of human beings is dependence. We are dependent on each other in this life. Whatever we do in life depends on another person either physically or mentally. Therefore, dependence in life makes it necessary for us to form relationships. You must realize that this is a crucial part of letting out your true self. Relationships integrally link themselves to our destiny. We, you see, are more than likely going to move in the direction of our relationships. This is why our first relationship in adult life, including family, must be with the

Creator. We are forever dependent on the Creator. When we form the right dependency on our God, then all other relationships will modify accordingly. Relationships require sharing as a natural component. This is why the importance of relationship determines our destiny. We naturally gravitate toward the people we share with the most. We first start in the family and then move to the larger world. However, we carry the same behavior we learned in our family of origin to our daily encounters. It is very important to realize relationship determines your destiny. In relationships, you are letting out your true self even when you are unaware. Sharing means more that just giving people things. It means that we are exchanging important things like our presence, our thoughts, and our feelings. In other words, your "me" is becoming like the persons with whom you are most in relationship. Therefore, self is the most important person we should be in relationship with before we form relationships with other people and things. If the self is not centered then the relationships we form will not be centered. There will always be an unstable quality in the relationship. The self, this is your true self, your "me," must have good experiences.

Experience, as we have seen above, is the food that produces individual growth. This growth is the outcome of values that provide energy for our wholeness. Moreover, most importantly, the need for wholeness energizes the desire for healthy personality. There is a need for wholeness in each of us. We cannot help but to seek wholeness. This wholeness wants to be let out in personality. This is the reason why we seek out experiences in the first place. We sense that experiences can make us whole. The need for wholeness is the main force behind our behavior. We did not put this desire for wholeness in us. This need for wholeness is part of the Creation. We, like all of Creation, seek completeness. Everything in Creation is seeking completeness or equilibrium. The drive for completeness is the same energy that drives us for personality growth. Integrity is the word we us to describe the complete connection of our personality. When the individual has integrity it simple means everything is connected together in the way it should be connected. Here, you must realize that integrity can be either positive or negative. In Incarnation Centered Spirituality, the drive for integrity is the same positive energy as the drive for completeness. There is a pattern of completeness for everything. The pattern of completion when properly connected results in growth. Significantly, everything in Creation seeks the fulfillment of completeness. Therefore, the trigger that keeps us looking for experiences that will give us the completeness we need is curiosity. When we are curious about the things in the world we are unable to remain static we must become active. We can see this in the toddler as it samples everything in its environment with its five senses to satisfy its mind. Mind is inquisitive by design. Mind is the measure of a person. The mind makes the person to become who he or she is. This is why the attitude is important. The attitude is a fixed mindset; therefore, it is important that you remain aware of your attitude. When the fixed mindset directs the individual then the individual has stopped thinking and is automatically reacting. Now, there is nothing wrong with automatically reacting. This could be the safest thing to do in times. However, when your mind is fixed to the extent that nothing new can enter your mind, then your personality is stunted. To prevent this you need to form a network with fellow travelers, which is relationship. However, a network is a practical relationship. Network helps the mind to keep examining its state of being. The network is a stimulus for the mind. This is why you carefully develop your network. Your network helps you to keep thinking in a forward direction. The tool of letting your real self in the context of unity out is the technique of Life that introduces you to kindred minds. Therefore, you must remember that it is all about the attitude in personality development. Moreover, the survival of your true self really depends on your attitude. Your attitude, though unbelievable as it may seem, really is regulated by your desire to let your true self out. We all have attitudes. However, contrary to what we believe about the fixed attitude it can be unfixed. Incarnation Centered Spirituality is really about learning how to unfix the attitude. This is how you learn to keep an open mind. An open mind is necessary for personality development. It is a survival strategy. Survival means more that just staying alive. It means saving your true self and your potential to develop your true self. This is why it is all about your attitude in personality development. Attitude sharpens your judgmental ability.

Judgment is the ability to discriminate. When we can make the best discrimination in life about the things in life then we are in a safe mode. The safe mode is freedom from contradictions in our judgments. This is why the safety valve of judgment is an open mind. We must overcome a great deal of obstacles in life and as we overcome the obstacles, we develop ethical judgmental skills. Ethics is the foundation of good judgment. Ethics is not something we create. Ethics is already part of the Creation. When God saw "that it was good" during the act of creating the universe, God was saying that there is an intrinsic good that determines all other good. This good is what we call ethics. Ethics is universal. What is good for one is good for all no matter where we may live. Morality may change from place to place but never ethics. This is why ethics is the foundation of judgment. Now here we are not talking about judgment in the sense of a court of law. Law is not ethical. Law should be ethical; however, in a court of law things must just be legal. Therefore, in life there is another standard of judgment. This standard is the same standard the

Creator used when He declared Creation to be good. In the heart of Creation, there is a good that we call ethics; it will remain, just like mathematics. Ethics is just part of Creation. You establish your personal balanced in life only when you make the sound judgment that stands on this universal good. Balance in your life, after all it is the reason for the safety valve of judgment, is for you to be who you are in this world. When we are balanced in life, we generate trust as a product of humility. Trust comes from the appearance of a person who has no hidden agenda. The person who seeks what is best for the next person is more likely to be trusted than a person who has self-seeking tendencies. We develop the attribute of balance, when seeking the good for other people in crisis. Consequently, crisis is the revealer of values. The value system of a person will always be revealed under pressure. A person's character is most likely to show up under pressure. The power of humility is effective in personal influence because the person who has the most humility is the one who is most likely trusted by others. When character and personality are alike, an attraction generates trust. Attraction is always the basis of influence.

Your physical, spiritual, and moral influence is readily apparent when you behave in any situation. What we do or say will reflect our true level of humility. Others can feel humility in this sense. Humility is not something you can show by personal effort. If you know that, you are showing humility then more than likely you are not humble. This is why the power of humility is so effective in personal influence. Letting out your true self is magnetic.

Magnetism is the power of attraction in metals. In addition, there is a magnetic attraction in the spiritual life. When we are spiritually developed beyond the normal way of life, which is more than likely no more than the natural way of living, we will become attractive to the people of the world. They will see an aura that is bright and attractive. Your memory of a lost harmony that has become alive in your soul will ignite your total Personality. Your "me" in you has a memory of a lost harmony that wants to get out. Truly, you are the product of your memory. We have selective memory. It is the choice of what we want to remember that makes us who we are. Your memory generates your drive for personality development. You remain slow and unmotivated until you develop drive in your life. This drive comes from your memory. Moreover, this drive makes you pick up your pace and move with more energy and deliberation. Your expectation ignites with possibilities. You have hope. Hope is expectation. When we expect something to happen, we look forward to it happening. Hope is really the blessing of memory. More, importantly, memory is more vital than written history, of all the things we have in our memory we have something to hope for rather than something to try to forget. This is why we must always try to keep hope alive. Hope is your memory that is always transforming and creating ways for letting out your true self in life. We dare not forget our past it is always our future. We remember our origins in the nation and in the family. Origin is the ground of our hope. Your "me" in you is the ground of hope.

Origin in your family never stops influencing your life because your "me" in you forever stays connected to family. We never forget our family members. In fact, we never stop looking for them in other people. No matter where we go our family members show up in other people. We have the same feeling for them that we had for the family member. Genetics, also, play a very important part in our development. We receive certain genes from our mothers and fathers that they received from their mothers and fathers. We inherit many things from our parents that influence us the rest of our lives. Therefore, we never outgrow our family. Characteristics that show up in the physical body come from the gene pool. We carry the same physical characteristics in our bodies that other members of our gene pool carried. This is in generations past. Our genetic family becomes larger than our nuclear family. The West considers ancestor worship to be paganism. Nevertheless, in the West, we practice it; the truth in fact is, we recognize that we are always part of our ancestors. However, we are, as we remember our ancestors, more stable in life. It is this inner connection with the family that the power of family never stops working in our lives. More importantly, you are aware of your inner connection of family through your "me" that is inside of you.

This connection keeps our will strong. The will is part of the dominant need of our personality. William Glasser has found that personality is created out of a "genetic need-strength profile that is unique for each of us."[16] We chose to act out of the basic needs such as power, belonging, freedom and fun according to which of these dominates.[17] It is the choice to act that we call the will. We all have will. When we are taking an action to accomplish something we are acting out of the will. The will is a great factor in personality development. When understood that the will is always under our control, it will become a great power for spiritual development. We will be more assertive. Assertiveness is often confused for aggressiveness. They are not the same things; assertiveness is positive action while aggressiveness is usually negative action. Assertiveness leaves another person feeling good about the situation. The well-developed personality has learned how to be assertive without being aggressive. When this happens, the other person will have a good impression about the assertive action. Character, as we have seen, is not personality. Character is the development of the value system in the person to the extent that the person will always act in such a way that the greatest good for the greatest number of people will always be the first consideration. Personality, on the other hand, is the character acting out which may be true of false. If the thinking and the feeling are well under control, the action is always the expression of the true character in the personality. Your objective is to make your character and your personality the same. This is your "me" inside of you. The image and the person become the same.

You must become your true image of your whole person. Image is the visible sign of the object. When we talk about the Image of God, we are talking about the Creator. We know God is a Spirit and no one has seen God. Nevertheless, we do know the attributes of God. There are certain attributes that of necessity must be Godly if there is a God. The Bible tells us about the attributes of God. When we accept the attributes of God, it is but a short stride to knowing the creative attributes of man. It must not be, that we take the attributes of man and apply them to God, simply because we have determined that there is a Supreme Being, and the attributes that we have, must first come from the Supreme Being. This is why divinity is the ultimate goal in the development of humanity. Transformation always changes us into divinity. Transformation in the human being is possible only because of the attributes of God. The personality transforms into the image of God. Divine nature is possible because personality transforms into a divinity that is always at the heart of Creation. Cosmic consciousness reveals goals that are in the human being. Your ultimate goal in the development of your personality is divinity. You become the personality that seeks freedom, justice, and identity in life. In fact, you become the personification of freedom, justice, and identity. This leads to a lifestyle discussed in Chapter 16 as the tool of Sacramentalism. This is your life commitment, as the Prophethood of black believers in the gospel of Jesus, to the African American struggle for freedom, justice, and identity.

Chapter 16

Living the Life of Sacramentalism

Hold out yo' light you heav'n boun' soldier,
Hold out yo' light you heav'n boun' soldier,
Hold out yo' light you heav'n boun' soldier,
Hold out yo' light you heav'n boun'soldier,
Let yo' light shine a-roun' de world.

Sacramentalism produces a life of dedication in the Path of the Via Transformativa. The above Negro spiritual expresses the Sacramentalism of the African American enslaved singers. They used the metaphor of the soldier holding out his light, to express the idea of a life consecrated to freedom, justice, and identity. Therefore, in the Path of the Via Transformativa, the technique of Life brings the tool of Sacramentalism to the level of a lifestyle of consecrated duty to live for freedom, justice, and identity. Thus, Sacramentalism means consecration to freedom, justice, and identity in this chapter. You, as the enslaved, sang in the above spiritual, are still heaven-bound soldiers. Therefore, it is your Sacramental duty to live with the knowledge that ultimate victory is freedom, justice, and identity. Moreover, you must live as if, you know that in life there is always something more than what you see. Therefore, always be in the process of looking for something of value to sacrifice your life for. It is true, in fact, it may be country, family, or tribe, but you will give your life with the idea that you are giving your life to some sacred person or ideal. The whole of religion is the outgrowth of this kind of thinking. We are born into the social web of sacrifice. However, worship is the closest thing to sacrifice. In fact, worship is a form of sacrifice. The Scripture tells us in Romans 12:1, "I beseech you, therefore, brethren, by the mercies of God, that ye present your bodies a living sacrifice, holy, acceptable unto God, which is your reasonable service." We are always worshipping in one way or another. Worshipping takes all kinds of forms. It just so happens that we in the Christian religion have forms of worship, which come from the Judeo-Christian tradition. Nevertheless, this does not make it essentially any different from other kinds of worship. In this sense, worship is worship. Duty, moreover, is a great part of worship. We think we have a duty to pay homage to the gods. This is a universal phenomenon. There is a worship tendency in the genetic makeup of human beings. It makes paying homage to the gods a natural part of being human. The difference in the religion of Jesus, however, is that this natural tendency transforms into spiritual consciousness of sacrificial living for freedom, justice, and identity. We know that we are seeking the Ultimate Being when we seek freedom, justice, and identity. Sacramentalism, of enslaved African Americans, as expressed in the previous Negro spiritual, leads to transformation. This transformation is the insight that truth is foundational to being. This is what enables you to live the sacramental life of seeking freedom, justice, and identity. Moreover, the knowledge that truth is foundational to being demands, a life of Sacramentalism as well. The Divine Being of Creation makes it possible for the human being in Creation to seek foundational truth. Therefore, New Birth is the name given to the transformation that comes from the conversion experience. You must realize that the Holy Spirit is the carrier of truth that is foundational to being. When we are born again, we receive a revelation about divine living. This is why the enslaved singers told the heaven-bound soldiers to hold out their lights. Light is truth.

This is why the light of sacramental insight becomes a part of the life of the believer in Jesus Christ. The sacraments of Baptism and Communion are for living the divine life of faith. There is not even a possibility that we could believe in Jesus Christ intellectually. An intellectual faith alone is incapable of leading us to the life of Sacramentalism in Incarnation Centered Spirituality.

Incarnation Centered Spirituality is a sacramental lifestyle. Seeking is more than an intellectual curiosity. It is the total search for Ultimate Reality. Ultimate Reality is something that has to be lived rather than something that is discovered. Therefore, sacramental living constitutes the search for living the life of Jesus in the Path of the Via Transformativa. Only the true believer knows that truth is foundational to divine being. Moreover, this truth compels the true believer to adapt to a lifestyle of sacramental living.

By faith, after all, is the surest way to experience ultimate goodness in life. Always, at the core of things goodness gives meaning to any situation. Nothing, therefore, is all bad; there is always a form of goodness present that makes us responsible. We are responsible for finding goodness in every situation. Our natural response is to seek for our self the best in a situation rather than to seek the good in a situation. Moreover, this is by far, the sin of human nature. It is this self-centeredness that constitutes sin. Surrender is the only way to overcome this tendency of self-centeredness. When we surrender to the God of the universe we, find the goodness at the core of the universe. We know the goodness because we know the God of goodness. Look at your expectations. Your expectations can never be higher than your knowledge of goodness. You will have experienced ultimate goodness when you experience the God of goodness. There is no other way you could have high expectations in this world unless you have experienced the goodness at the core of the universe. When we know that God became a person in order to call us back to divinity, then we know the goodness of the universe. This is why, in Christianity, God came as a baby. There is nothing purer than a baby. When we look at Baby Jesus in the manger, we are looking at purity. Moreover, this is the revelation of the goodness at the core of the universe that leads to transformation. This is what we mean by the statement, "You can't beat God's giving." God has given us Jesus in a manger, born of a virgin, purity personified. The five-fold path of Incarnation Centered Spiritual is the journey to the goodness of wholeness as affirmed in the birth of Jesus.

You, moreover, must know that truth is the extension of the beautiful. As a result, the conformation of truth is beauty. The two elements in life are the same. Nothing is true until there is confirmation and there is no confirmation unless it is also beautiful. Sacramentalism is the doing of truth. Therefore, its confirmation is the beauty of love. Love is the way of God. God is love. It is love that we are really seeking in life. It is when we seek love that we find truth. Truth dwells with love. Love is the outward expression of truth in action. When we discover that, our interior self is the cluster of beauty, truth, and love, we have also found the basis of faith. It is this cluster that contains the force of God. Love is a beautiful expression of Incarnation Centered Spirituality. When we walk the Path of the Via Transformativa, we are walking in love. Love is the radiant light that illuminates the darkness. We can see the path of Sacramentalism in the divine light of love only because we have the innate beauty of truth in our inner self to guide our steps. When we lose our way, the light comes on in our souls and alerts us with an unacceptable noise that shakes us out of our sleep. However, silence follows this noise. Therefore, we want only to be in this silence. It is at this point that we become silent in our souls. Silence is a divine zone where we hear only the voice of God. The voice of God becomes celestial music to our ears. This celestial music is the same music the angels sang at the birth of the Holy Child. When we hear this celestial music, Holiness permeates all things with a beauty that leaves us speechless. Moreover, it is a feeling of captivation. We are overwhelmed by the feeling of being a creature. However, this is a good feeling because it makes us know that God is our Creator. It takes us back to our origins. Sacramentalism is about origins.

For you, origin is more than just the beginning of things in Incarnation Centered Spirituality. An origin is more about the directions of things than it is about beginnings. The origin of things makes them sacred. Thus, all things are scared because all things originate from God. Humanity changed sacred into secular. God only knows sacred. Moreover, purpose is the reason things originate. Therefore, only God can give things purpose. Purpose makes things sacred in the world. Moreover, from God's point of view, all things have purpose, but from the human point of view, things are secular. Things are sacred to human beings when we discover their purposes to God. This is why we are to give honor to the purpose of things. Purpose is God's will. When we disregard the purpose of things we are also disregarding the sacredness of things, and we are also disregarding the will of God. The Creator is more than a distant maker of things. We are the maker of things but God is the Creator of things. Sacramentalism in Incarnation Centered Spirituality is living according to the will of God, with the purpose of freedom, justice, and identity. The Creator gives things purpose; however, the maker of things uses the purpose of things to make things for practical use. This usually means art. Therefore, in the final analysis there is no such thing as art for art's sake, spiritually speaking. All art serves a practical purpose already in the scheme of things. It is the authenticity of the original purpose that makes a work of art a masterpiece. Art is a masterpiece when it serves a purpose that is already in the work of art which the human artist did not put in the work. The Creator alone has the right to give purpose. You must see that this built-in purpose by the Creator is why all things are sacred. The life of sacramental living must be a sacred masterpiece.

Sacramentalism in Incarnation Centered Spirituality is scientific. Science is confidence in the precision of Creation. Science does not make Creation stable. The stability of Creation makes science possible. If there were no precise predictability in the nature of things there could be no science. The law of physical nature is the same law of the spiritual nature. There is only one law. The law is the same above as below. It is in this regard that no science is free of faith. Scientists have faith in the laws of nature. Scientists' faith stops at the spiritual things; however, they err in this kind of behavior because law is spiritual. Trust in God is not but a short step to trust in Creation. The Creation speaks of God. The Creation is the first witness of the divine. When we look at the Creation we know that there is a Creator. Things don't just create themselves. The scientist is useful to humanity in this regard. Scientists know that nature can be trusted. But what is even more important is they know that nature did not create itself. This is the sense in which Sacramentalism is scientific. You can base your Sacramentalism on the stability of Creation. Moreover, you can anticipate the outcome of your life. Anticipation in Creation is a great act of confidence in the stability of Creation. Even earthquakes and storms can be anticipated because we know that there is stability in natural law. This is the basis of Sacramentalism. Now, Sacramentalism in Incarnation Centered Spirituality is not nature worship. Nevertheless, it is a life based on the God of nature, with a clear understanding that we, too, are nature. In Sacramentalism God is more than a prime mover. God is the Creator of heaven and earth. We look at the stars and know that there is a God that deserves respect and honor. Thus we worship God! Our anticipation is really about the God of Creation. We know who the Creator is and therefore we know what life is all about. Life is all about living as though there is a Creator who manifested himself in the Incarnation, Crucifixion, Resurrection, and the Ascension of Jesus. This is what Sacramentalism is about in Incarnation Centered Spirituality. It is about a life of submission in a constant act of worship and awe.

You must have an attitude of awe and wonder. This is the feeling of the great shock of being. When we look at the Creation, in its splendor, we are struck with awe. The wonder is the gift of the Creator that contributes to the transformation. When we lose the ability to have wonder about the mystery of life we have lost the sacred feeling of the presence of God. The wonder in life is the engine of Art and Science. Sacramentalism is the outward expression of wonder. It is this wonder that we call religion. All religion can be traced back to wonderment. Prayer is the attitude of awesomeness. It is this attitude that makes us bow to the Creator. We learned who the Creator is from the Old Testament. It is also from the Old Testament that we learned that the God of Creation deserves our prayers. The Old Testament characters showed us how to relate to God with a life of prayer. Yet, it is from the New Testament where we learn that the God of Creation is not some faraway being. We learn, moreover, that the God of Creation is as personal as a father. This is what Jesus told us to say when he taught the disciples to pray, "Our Father." Therefore, communion is the way we stay in contact with the Lord of life. When we are in communion we are in contact with the Holy Trinity. This is what calls you and sustains you in a life of Sacramentalism. There is not much practical difference between Communion and Sacramentalism. Communion is an act that is grounded in Sacramentalism. Sacramentalism is also an idea that calls for Communion. It is the idea of Sacramentalism that operates in the act of Communion. There is no real Communion without Sacramentalism. The experience of Communion and Sacramentalism is the attitude of awesomeness that leads to wholeness in life. This attitude is a life of Communion with the Creation grounded on a Sacramentalism based in Jesus Christ. You must learn that Sacramentalism, Communion, and Fellowship are the same. The tool of Sacramentalism unifies.

You must understand that fellowship is the ability to stay in relationship with God as a believer. This is using the tool of Sacramentalism in the Path of the Via Transformativa for wholeness. We are able to stay in fellowship because we practice a Communion that is based on a Sacramentalism we learned from the life and teachings of Jesus Christ. "As often," said Jesus, "as you do this do it in remembrance of me." When there is a true fellowship, there is true agreement. We are in agreement with Jesus Christ. This agreement is learned from Jesus' relationship with the Father. We imitate Jesus. This is what a true disciple does. This imitation is what holds the fellowship together. Following Jesus is a spiritual art that must be learned each generation. Your determination to imitate Jesus as an artist is your Sacramentalism. This is the evidence that there is a true following. When there is a true following, the imitation is identical to the one followed. There is no difference in the way the disciple and the Teacher relate to the Creator. Jesus called it being a good steward. Good stewardship is possible only when the fellowship and the followship of Jesus are compatible. Stewardship is trust with the treasures of the household of God, which by the way is the Creation. This is the meaning of living out of the abundant treasure of commitment. Commitment to God by receiving Jesus Christ as Savior is also a commitment to fellowship, to be a following person, and a steward of God's household.

The Godhead is an interconnection that defines unity. It is upon the unity of the Father, Son, and Holy Spirit that all unity is possible. There is no other paradigm that better defines unity. This unity has neither separation nor disharmony. The Godhead union is a compatible relationship that can be seen in the history of human salvation. In fact, salvation history reveals the perfect union of the Father, Son, and Holy Spirit. It is this union that binds us to the interconnection in life. To be out of unity with Creation is to be in sin against the Creator. Furthermore, there is a built in logic in human thought that informs us when we are in unity with Creation. Thought is a necessary part of human beings. We cannot be human and be without thought, no matter how illogical. In fact, even an insane person has a fundamental logic to his or her insane thinking and behavior. When we can detect the meaning of insane thought patterns, then we can make sense out of insane behavior. This is true because we all are bound by the interconnection of life. Feeling is the most irrational part of the personality, in the sense that it is not designed to think. It is, however, a good indicator of our environmental surroundings. We can trust what we feel in the sense that feelings call attention to our needs. However, this attention comes from our intellect. Nevertheless, thinking, feeling, and acting are interconnected. We are responsible for knowing when to respond with thinking, feeling or acting. Your responsibility is the right reaction to the sensed presence.

We respond to something that is there. Thus, there can be no responsibility unless there is something to respond to in our environment. The word responsibility is used so much with the sense of duty, until we forget that it first means to react to our environment. There may be a sense of duty attached, but the first meaning is to react to stimulus. The original stimulus is the Creator. We are always responding to God in one way or another. Living in a world of materialism often robs us of this knowledge. This is why spirituality is important in life. Renewal is possible because we can respond to God. It is the call to renewal at all times from the Creator that keeps us responding. Fulfillment is the sign that we have responded correctly. When we sense a feeling of fulfillment, we also feel responsible. Remember that Sacramentalism is consecration. Furthermore, this is what consecration means. It means that we have responded in a sacramental way to the Creator. Only the Creator can consecrate us. The God of Creation consecrates us to a way of responding to the call for unity with the Godhead. This is why consecration is assurance in life. When you have a feeling of assurance, you have a sense of consecration. When you can say God is in heaven and all is well in the world, you have reached a level of transformed consciousness. In this state of consciousness, the flow of divinity connects you to the Ultimate Reality--the Creator.

Flow is the best way to describe what it means to be in communion with the Creator. This is important to mention again because it is necessary for you to know that flowing is the experience of communion. We realize that all reality is flowing from and back to God. Being aware, of this flow, is being aware of the communion with the Creator. We cannot get out of Creation. We can only be in flow with Creation. Harmony is the experience of the wellness in your soul that has no false movements. When there is no wasted energy, then there is perfect harmony. We must learn how to conserve energy not only in the physical world but also in the spiritual world. The truth is all is energy. Thus, energy is always in the flow of becoming something else. Below the atomic structure is the quantum that is becoming what thought is directing it to become. This is why we must know about the flow of Creation. Communication with the Creation in our souls is a normal thing. There is a form of communication that can be called reflection that helps us to talk to nature. This is because there is life in all things. Life may be more expressed in one thing than another, but there is only one life. Life is life. All living organisms possess the same life. If we take the time we can talk to the life in a tree, as well as, the life in a rabbit. Life is life. All life can communicate with other life, if we are alert enough to catch the flow of life. This is the essence of Sacramentalism.

In Sacramentalism, there is a level of contemplation. This level makes communication with life possible. Contemplation is a gift from God. We are able to communicate with God constantly when we have reached the level of contemplation. Contemplative ability comes from an effort to reach the level of talking with God in the Spirit. When we can talk with God, while doing other things, then we have reached a level of spirituality that the average person never reaches. They could however, if they put forth the effort. God wants us to talk with Him more than talking to Him. Initiation into the contemplative life comes after a long hard struggle to live a sacramental life. This initiation is not done in a cult or with some other kind of religious group. It comes simply as we learn how to talk with God. We will need some experienced spiritual person to guide us, but not to possess us. Only God should possess us. Students of Spirituality must first learn that life is a vocation of prayer. However, prayer is talking with God. When this is learned, then the next step is to become aware of the need for constant repentance. With the vocation of prayer goes the vocation of repentance. This is what Sacramentalism really is all about. It is a life of prayer and repentance expressed in joy and praises to God. Only then can we know the oneness of nature. It is at this time that we can answer God's question to Job, "Who is this that darkens counsel by words without knowledge?" We can shout, "I was in the flow of your thoughts." This is the gospel. You see, we have never been without God.

Gospel is more that good news. When we say gospel, we think of the English translation of good news, or Godspeed. But the mystery of the gospel gets lost in this translation. What really is good news is the fact that we don't have to take this definition of gospel. We can enter into the experience and know the meaning from the inside. This is what the scripture tells us in Ephesians where Paul talks about the positional and the experiential relationships of the believer. A positional relationship is the relationship that we already have in Christ while the experiential relationship is the daily encounters in the world. When we enter into the gospel we will sense the universality of salvation. We know that the whole Creation is in the process of becoming new. We also know that the universality of salvation is also a particular salvation. This means that salvation is one person at a time and only one person at a time. A person's sense of need makes the person aware of the universality of salvation. There is emptiness in the soul that keeps crying out to God. This outcry is the longing for wholeness. The soul knows when it is broken. It is this knowledge of brokenness that makes us know that there is a universal salvation of wholeness. Nature is broken. With the Fall of Man in Adam, all nature was broken. This state of brokenness calls for a universal salvation. The scripture says, "For the creation was subjected to futility, not of its own will, but because on Him who subjected it, in hope that creation itself also will be set free from its slavery to corruption into freedom of the glory of the children of God. For we know that the whole creation groans and suffers the pains of childbirth together until now [Romans 8:20-22]." The tool of Sacramentalism leads to good works. In Chapter 17, you will learn what good works mean in Incarnation Centered Spirituality on the Path of the Via Communitiva. The Path of the Via Communicativa with the Technique of Enlightening the community.

PATH V

THE VIA COMMUNITIVA, ENLIGHTENMENT FOR THE BELOVED COMMUNITY

Chapter 17

Producing Good Works
For Solutions In Life

Live-a humble, humble, Lord; Humble
Yo'self, de bell done ring.
Live-a humble, humble, Lord; Humble
Yo'self de bell done ring

The Path of the Via Communitiva is the pathway of enlightening the community, to continue the goals of the civil rights struggle, by ushering in the Beloved Community. On the Path of the Via Communitiva, enlightenment is the Technique for building the community. The first thing that you want to produce is the tool of good works that grew out of the Path of the Via Transformativa. On this path, you learned how to live to teach the community how to live the spiritual life as the life of Jesus. Life is the fourth technique of the Turner E.A.G.L.E. Technique in the Path of the Via Transformativa. This life is the Life of Jesus. The enslaved singers of the spiritual, "Humble Yo'self de Bell Done Ring," sang about living the life of Jesus in order to produce good works. They sang about doing the good works of being humble like Jesus. Good works are the true products of Christian Spirituality. In Christian Spirituality, you live the example of Jesus as good works. An example is always the best visual aid for teaching. Remember in God's Word, Jesus told his disciples to follow him instead of telling them to worship him. When you continue on the Path of the Via Communitiva, you begin to use the technique of Enlightenment of the Turner E.A.G.L.E. Technique; you have mastered living the life of Jesus in the spiritual journey up to now. Consequently, you are now the model of Jesus. After all, the model for living, the spiritual life, is the Life of Jesus. Moreover, the model of Jesus is the example of good works. This is why Incarnation Centered Spirituality is a great form of spirituality for doing good works. Doing good works begins with faith as the very attitude of Jesus. Jesus did not do anything that He did not believe the Father was instructing Him to do. Jesus left the outcome of His actions up to the Father. You too must leave the outcome of your actions up to the Father; this is the call to faith, which in fact is, the life of Jesus. You leave the outcome up to the Father. Your mission is the goal of enlightening the community to the call of God to do good works. Your mission is to do the good works that Jesus came to do--the works of redemption. His will was to do the will of his Father. It is the will of the Father to build the Beloved Community.

You must understand that God's will is the driving force of the redemptive business of God. Moreover, the driving force of redemption is why good works are always a matter of God's business. You must understand, as good works are according to the will of God, it is always a matter of God's business being done in history. You must never lose this historical perspective of the way redemption works. This way of redemption determines your direction as well as your means and manners. You see, it does matter how you do good works. Thus, this means that when you do good works to meet your needs, you do not prevent others from meeting their needs. You must be sure that you are using the technique of Enlightenment, on the Path of the Via Communitiva. This is the only way that you can be sure you are doing your Heavenly Father's business. This is what Jesus meant by doing His Father's will. When you are in your own will, you are on the wrong path. Your practice of Incarnation Centered Spirituality keeps you on the right path. When we are going in the right direction, good works are a matter of God's business, because your good works and your direction are identical. This is why you learned the art of obedience.

Obedience is the only way you can do good works. There is a foundation upon which good works are established. This foundation, in fact, is also your source of good works. This foundation is obedience to the will of God. When it is the will of God, then obedience is your first line of defense against the forces that try to prevent you from doing good works. This supports the underlying principle about why conversion is first necessary for doing good works. If there is no conversion then there are no good works, and there is no effort to build the Beloved Community. Your New Birth gives you the ability to do good works as Jesus. If there is no conversion then there are no good works, and there is no effort to build the Beloved Community. Your New Birth is the continuation of Creation. Creation is the source of the pattern for good works. We are after all still involved in the creative process of God. God is still in the act of Creation. God's Word keeps all things on course. Therefore, the foundation for your growth in good works is your act of obedience to God's Word. Good works are deliverance for building the Beloved Community. The enlightenment of the community is an act of deliverance that results in the Beloved Community. However, deliverance is the good work of God through Jesus Christ.

You are still involved in the work of deliverance in Jesus Christ. Try to understand that in the 21st century many African Americans are still trapped in a system of oppression living under the White supremacy doctrine that still operates throughout U.S. institutions. African Americans still experience injustice throughout the justice system, and many are still living with an identity problem that causes them to remain ignorant of their own history. These African Americans still need their deliverance. You must always seek ways to deliver these captives from this world to the Beloved Community. You can see the glory of deliverance in your own life. This glory is the destination of traveling on the Via Communitiva. All the awesome things that we do in the community we do to the glory of God. If what you are doing is not to the glory of God, then it is not good works. Good works are their own authentic proof that they are the works of God. After all, they are good works because they always produce good works of deliverance in the community. If a good work does not produce good results then it is not of God. All good works must be about the business of delivering the captives from the bondage of self-imposed slavery, injustice, and the death of a lack of identity. Good works release those held captive.

Release is also a part of deliverance. It is not until a captive soul is released from that which is holding it captive, that it can be delivered. This is the intention of liberation. Liberation is more than a political act. It is first a spiritual act. The setting free of the captive is the liberation of the soul. Responsibility is the overall purpose of liberation. Those held captive must also take responsibility for their own liberation. This may sound like a contradiction of faith. Nevertheless, even faith means that there is responsibility for believing and acting according to that belief. Birthing is the best analogy for describing liberation. It is the responsibility of the baby to make its way out of the birth channel even with help from the mother. The baby works to get here. So then, you can see from this example, good works are liberation for responsibility. You can also see that European missionary work did not liberate. This is the blemish on the European missionary work during the time of exploration, colonization, and exploitation of the nations of other peoples.

The European missionary concept of redemption caused much suffering, among the victims, who were supposed to be redeemed, by the Christian religion, as taught by individuals in the guise of missionaries. Christian religion is full of horrible acts of the missionary. The colonial powers could not have been as successful as they were if not for the missionary. This is not to say that it was the intention of the missionary to be the point man of colonization and exploitation. Nevertheless, this is the fact of the matter. Many natives of the countries invaded by European people have a lasting picture of the missionary and his Bible. This is why the intention of the mind is the most important thing in the enterprise of the human being. The mind of the missionary is very important. When we look at the mind of the missionary according to the writings left behind, we see that there was a sense that they were bringing civilization to the heathens, so they could be used by the colonial powers, to do their biding. This kind of thinking has a built in flaw that leads to mass killings and slavery. Elemental forms of anything must be examined in order to understand the nature of the whole thing. This is why the mind of the missionary is important. We must understand that good works must never lead to the mass killings and slavery that the missionary work produced in Christian History. This is why good works must always have with it an element of repentance for those doing good works.

Repentance is the change of direction. It is turning from that which is not God to that which is God in a true faith. Only when there is repentance is there a possibility of good works. There can be no good works until there is repentance. The only good work an unsaved person can do is the act of repentance. The only good work that a saved person can do is the act of continuous repentance. This is why a vocation of prayer is, in fact, a real vocation of repentance. Everyday you should be in the act of repentance. In fact, your whole life should be an act of repentance.

Responding to the call of God is an act of repentance. God has not called us as just a one-time act, but rather, God is calling us. This means that God is always in the act of calling us. There is a constant call of God to good works on your life. Respecting the call of God is not a one-time thing. It is a vocation of prayer. Your life becomes a vocation of prayer when you are constantly in the act of living out your calling in life. This calling cannot be accomplished without a vocation of prayer. There is a formula for this life of prayer. It is your receptive response to the calling of God for repentance. This response requires that you surrender your control. One of the two modes of consciousness is the receptive mode, which according to Urban T. Holmes, is one of association, surrender, institution, and surprise. "It operates in a world of symbol, ritual, and story. It is an often neglected function which, by diffusing our awareness, allows the possibility of new or expanded consciousness. It is a difficult form or sense of experience for a people socialized, to think for control."[18] This calling to a vocation of repentance produces the good works. The formula is for building the Beloved Community with the whole body as the focal point of liberation.

The body is an example of good works because body has a sense of completion. The body is the perfect sense of good works because it represents the fulfillment of what is the nature of that which is to be done. When good works appear, it will represent the body of Christ. The Body of Christ will be a unified purpose that functions to produce good works. Moreover, this blueprint for good works will have the total objective of the good works that builds the Beloved Community. Purpose is the outcome that determines the quality of good works. There must never be just sentimentality as the outcome of good works. The good works are the answer to necessity.

Necessity is always the final cause for good works done in life. If there is no necessity for doing what is done then, it is better to leave it alone. When we do anything, it ought to have a quality of necessity about it. For example, when we are feeding the hungry as good works, it should be necessary. Just because a person wants to eat, is no reason to feed the person. Feeding the hungry at times may not be good works. If there is no necessity, the output is flawed. Overlooked in this case is the necessity for learning to produce one's own food. The right output is food production. Output is a very real part of good works. The input we get from circumstances that call for good works will always have the necessary information we need to complete the output of works; there is also this kind of feeding experience of good works in every activity. Everything that is important to do will have the nature of feeding about it. Jesus says to Peter, "Feed My Sheep" even when he was talking about preaching and teaching. Starvation makes the feeding process a good measuring device for necessity. This illustration is useful because the example of necessity determines all good works. Doing what is unnecessary is out of balance. It is necessary for you to teach the community to strive for balance in everything, especially in freedom, justice, and identity.

Essentially, balance is justice. Justice addresses the issue of balance. If there is no sense of balance then justice is not accomplished. Justice is accomplished when the feedback is a sense of balance. Therefore, feedback helps us to know when there is balanced justice. The people involved will always know if justice has been served. It is possible that there will be those who want revenge instead of justice. For these people justice is impossible. Nevertheless, the very fact that they want revenge, instead of justice, is good feedback for establishing balance. The only corrective to revenge is justice. The good work of justice is corrective. Good work is curative. Corrective is the best sign that justice has been served. If the judgment does not give the sense of a corrective outcome, then there is no real sense of justice. In the final analysis it all comes back to balance in the sense of justice. Balance produces a feeling of fairness. Fairness is essential to community. The Path of the Via Communitiva using the Technique of Enlightenment for the community about fairness ushers in the Beloved Community.

Fairness is the sincere desire for equality. When we think there is fair distribution, we think we have been treated equally. This shows the desire for equality. A sense of fair treatment is important. Self-fulfillment is the result of fair treatment. When we feel like we have been fulfilled with a sense of equality, then we have a sense of self-respect and of self-worth. Your desire behind equality can really be traced back to a sense of fulfillment. Contributions are the result of the way we feel about our self. When we feel good about our self, we are more than likely to make good contributions to the community in which we live. You would do well to understand that a good sense of equality is necessary because it relates directly to good works. Moreover, stability, which is necessary in every endeavor of good works, is necessary in community. When the community is stable, it has the ability to do the things necessary for good works. This is why you must strive for stability in the community. The most important thing you can do for those in your immediate presence is to impart knowledge that results in stability. However, this knowledge will come from a constant search for information about the things you think important for good works. You can never stop searching for information about the things you have been called to do in life. Giving, too, is an important part of good works. If we are not a knowledge-giving person, then we are not a nurturing person. Therefore, if we are neither knowledge-giving nor nurturing, we are not ready to do good works for the community. Good works really do come down to nurturing the community with knowledge. This is how you bring connection to the community.

Connection is the most important thing you can do as good works. You first connect with Jesus Christ. Clearly if there is no connection with Jesus Christ, then there is no possibility of doing good works. Good works are the connection between Jesus Christ and you using the Technique of Enlightenment on the Path of Via Communitiva. This connection is the beginning of your networking for the Beloved Community. When you build a good network, you will have completed the most important part of doing good works. You must realize that it is very selfish for you to try to make it alone in the community. The lone traveler is usually a person who has trouble working with others. The appreciation of others is your most important possession when it comes to building networks. The first thing you must have is an appreciation for the people with whom you are trying to network. Network in this sense means more than just hanging out together. It means that you share a lifeline. This lifeline is the very organism through which the vital life forces of the network flow.

Interestingly, treatment from people usually reflects how we are treating people. When people smile at us, it is because they have seen a smile on our face. We are always telling people how we want them to treat us by the way we treat them. This is what it means to give respect. Jesus told us, "We should treat others the way we want others to treat us." This works! It sets the tone of every encounter we have with other people. The good works are possible because you have a very strong need of good works from others. We know that if we were in the same circumstances we would want somebody to treat us the way we are treating those whom we are serving. Equality, in this situation, means much more than just an ethical concept. It means a relationship that serves to bring about the atmosphere that is necessary to do good works. Always reflecting on the work done will reveal if there was the kind of behavior that would result in good works. This is true because even if we accomplish the work, it may not be a good work. This is the perfect example of when the means must meet the ends. It matters how others feel about what we have done for them. This enlightens community. In fact, the concept of community is first.

Community is a concept important for doing good works. The concept of community grows larger everyday. Transportation and technology are turning the world into a single community. It is true now that the world is a village. Hence, you must keep your mind opened to the idea of globalization as community development.

The pain in Africa is the same tension you feel in the United States of America. It is truer now than ever before that you are your brother's keeper. Survival is now a global affair. The diseases that kill in a small village in the Congo are just an air flight away from your home. Your survival depends on how you view globalization. As stated throughout this book, concepts and ideas are more complex in meaning than they would appear. Globalization is no exception. Globalization is about much more than trade. It is about survival. The world today is more that just a globe on which you live; it has evolved into a unified system as never before. Get a deep understanding that your community is still planet earth and that the planet is not growing any larger. On the other hand, it is getting smaller because modern technology makes us all neighbors. This is a difficult idea for some of us to grasp. Even so, it is an idea that is a real part of good works. You must strive to enlighten the Beloved Community that non-violent resistance is more than a political strategy; it is a survival strategy for the entire human race. In Chapter 18, you will learn how to use non-violent resistance as a tool for building the Beloved Community in the Path of the Via Communitiva.

Chapter 18

Teaching the Value of
Nonviolent Resistance

Didn't my Lord deliver Daniel,
Deliver Daniel, deliver Daniel,
Didn't my Lord deliver Daniel,
And why not every man.

This spiritual, "Didn't My Lord Deliver," implies that nonviolent resistance is the natural response to violence. The enslaved singers were well aware that violence would never help them to achieve their goals of freedom, justice, and identity. They looked into the life of Daniel and saw what God intended in Creation. They saw that Daniel was protected by the overriding harmony of Creation because he was in the will of the Creator. There is an inherent order and harmony that God must protect as Creation, in the life of Daniel, as his story unfolds. Essentially, Creation is community. Community is the harmony of environment and people living in cooperative unity. Harmony is the main ingredient of the Beloved Community. Preacher-activist, Dr. Martin L. King, Jr. showed us that we could best achieve this harmony through nonviolent resistance. Michael N. Nagler wrote a book, *The Search for a Nonviolent Future*, which helps us understand that violence is unnatural and nonviolence is natural. We must first have a vision of harmony before we can work for nonviolent resistance. When we can see the lack of friction and the state of peace then we have something toward which to work. Nagler says, "Nonviolence has two faces, that of cooperating with good and that of noncooperating with evil."[19] The first lesson about nonviolence we must learn in life, is that nonviolence, is the normal way of the human being, and that violence, is learned behavior. We must sense that nonviolent resistance is a natural response to violence. We will then strive for peace, which is natural.

The peaceful environment that lurks just behind the violence, that we sense as unnatural is really the natural condition of life. Peace is natural. Isaiah said that the ultimate harmony in life is coming when, "The wolf also shall dwell with the lamb, The leopard shall lie down with the young goat. The calf and the young lion and the fatling together; And a little child shall lead them [Isaiah 11:6]." Peace is the absence of violence. However, this peace will not come until we learn that peace is the natural order of things. You are on the Path of the Via Communitiva to explore the peace of the nonviolent resistor. Moreover, peace is the product of refusing to accept the idea that violence is the natural way of things. This is how you work for the creation of harmony in the world. You sense the possibility of unity through nonviolence resistance.

Unity is the goal of reconciliation. Reconciliation is the absence of struggle between two parties. When we have been reconciled to God, then we are reconciled to our self, to one another, and to nature. However, today, we are destroying our natural environment because we are out of harmony with it. We are out of harmony with the Creator. Harmony is the evidence that there has been an act of reconciliation. Harmony makes it unnecessary to struggle against nature. Spiritually, we recognize that we are part of nature. Forgiveness becomes easier when we realize this fact. We have a great deal of negative feelings against nature and against our self, which makes us strike out at nature and at others. In fact, this simple act of forgiveness is the beginning of harmony. This illustrates why nonviolent resistance must be free of hatred. As a result, we seek the original peace in nonviolent resistance. The desire for peace is the desire for originality.

Original peace is the natural state of things. The original state of things does not cause the violence and oppression we face in racism throughout the world. Original peace is not the reason that we are afraid of each other. Racism is nothing but the outward expression of violence, which is the contradiction of the original purpose for Creation. When the dominant group practices racism, it is nothing more than a method of controlling the natural resources. This control takes the form of reducing others to a state of inferiority in order to justify the treatment used to keep the other group at a distance and under control. Inferiority is a false sense of self imposed on the oppressed group. There is no way the oppressed group can rise above this stamp of inferiority in the eyes of the dominant group. Inferiority is the basis of the racism that African Americans experience in the United States. Control is the rationale used by those who seek to be the dominant group. The method used most effectively to practice racism is the use of the ideal of *utopia*. This false ideal is the primary reason behind the extermination of races believed to be standing in the way of progress toward an ideal society. The utopian ideas of Western civilization have led to the exploration, exploitation, and colonization of the world based on the Western concept of racial superiority.

The concept of racial superiority, therefore, is the raw material of social chaos. This raw material of racial superiority causes unnatural violence among the peoples of the world. The people characterized as inferior will experience the violence of the group that thinks it is superior. Therefore, your nonviolent resistance must resist this form of violence, through the knowledge in your inner self, that God created all men in His own Image. Ignorance of your true self is a great aid to keeping this chaos going as a natural state of things. Your ignorance of the truth in your inner self is the ultimate tool used by White supremacy advocates to keep you powerless and under control. You need to realize that you have the Ultimate Reality of the Ground of Being in your inner self. Nonviolent resistance overcomes this ignorance. Ignorance leads to fear. Fear is the overriding force that operates in the sphere of chaos. Fear ignites the raw material of social chaos. Nonviolent resistance confronts fear and social chaos. There is an ethical element in nonviolent resistance that is at the very heart of Creation.

The ethical element in Creation is the real reason people reject violence in society. There is a sense of indignation that develops when a person sees outright violence towards other people. They react by trying to bring a stop to the violence, usually by using more violence. This indignation is necessary, but more violence is an unnatural response. If however, it were not for this sense of indignation, there would be no reaction against violence. Nevertheless, this reaction of indignation must be nonviolent. Moral rectitude is a powerful sense of right and wrong that will not let you stand by and let violence against powerless people continue. Improvement comes only when indignation is present. If you do not feel a sense of outrage, you will never seek improvement in life. You will never have a sense of indignation. Indignation is the energy necessary for change. Most of the changes for the better in history have come because of the indignation of an outraged person. The history of Christian Spirituality is filled with people outraged against the violent conditions under which people had to live. This honorable history of nonviolent resistors, beginning with Jesus, includes such names too as the Apostles, the African American freedom fighters, such as Harriet Tubman, Frederick Douglass, Medgar Evers, Dr. Martin L. King, Jr., and many others. Again, nonviolent resistance is an agency of change. It is that sense of the otherness in Creation that makes us identify with a power higher than the powers that seek to control others.

This sense of otherness is the origin of religion. Religion is always about the sense of the otherness of Creation. We sense that there is a power beyond humanity. When we sense that there is a greater being than we are, then we tend to develop a form of worship toward this supernatural being, which makes us sensitive to the violence in life. The real thing we are seeking when we attach a form of worship to the supernatural being is wholeness. We are striving to bring things into a state of oneness. Wholeness is that state of self that we sense when we have found unity in the oneness in Creation. Wholeness is the desire we seek in the oneness. You need to unite with this oneness in order to obtain your own personal wholeness. Your sense of the oneness is your awareness that God is outside of His Creation. Because of your sense of otherness, you can meet violence in life with nonviolent resistance. This is the real value of religion. This value determines our acts of nonviolent resistance for bringing community out of chaos. This is the true meaning of receiving the Kingdom of God. We never become immune to violence. This is possibly the meaning of receiving the Kingdom of God as a little child. We keep the little child's simple immediate response, or what the sophisticated adult calls naiveté, to cruelty and violence with a direct act of nonviolent resistance.

The practice of nonviolent resistance is to prevent you from losing your own sense of compassion in an insensitive world. A conscious act of nonviolent resistance helps you to win your own personal battle warring between compassion and vengeance in your own soul. Moreover, the practice of nonviolent resistance addresses the eternal opposition between freedom and slavery, or destruction and preservation. Even more importantly, the practice of nonviolent resistance demonstrates the worldview that reflects the belief that compassion is more than sentimentality. Nonviolent resistance is rather a practical act to preserve the ideal of the Beloved Community that every individual regardless of age, gender, or race has a role to play in the scheme of things, and that we need others in order to be our best self collectively and individually. Continuing with this line of reasoning, we see that nonviolent resistance is rooted in humanity as the highest value in life. Greater still, our own self-image directly connects to nonviolent resistance. We are, in fact, our brother's keeper. This idea helps us to recognize the unique value of every life, regardless of life form, through embracing the connection with all of life.

Nonviolent resistance in Incarnation Centered Spirituality is a spirituality of compassion freed of feelings of sentimentality. It contradicts violence as a way of life. It confronts the violence that seeks to assimilate life into a two-dimensional uniformed existence, enslaved to a self-defined master race, to do its bidding. Nonviolent resistance in this regard is compassionate action designed to remain free in order to express the God given possibilities of human life given by the Creator. This nonviolent resistance meets violence with a forgiving love; it significantly touches the humanity in the violent person that permits a brief sense of rebirth, as a human being. It awakens a consciousness toward compassion of freedom, justice, and identity. This compassion of non-violent resistance is the path of enlightening the Beloved Community with the compassion of nonviolent resistance. This form of enlightening the community is to lead the community to a wide-awake effort to elevate nonviolent resistance to a natural level of human response. The violent people of history have tucked it away from our sight, in order to conceal that nonviolence is our real heritage. We must become active recruiters of nonviolent resistors to establish nonviolent resistance as the normal spiritual force of nature. We must make compassion, the norm of our spiritual life.

Compassion compelled me to become actively involved in the resistance to inferior education. In 1965, I refused to sign a letter stating that the African American students were not ready to integrate the public schools due to their inferior level of education. Rather than sign this letter under pressure, I resigned the position. Compassion compelled me, to become actively involved in the protest, of the Prince George's County Ministers for Peaceful Integration, while serving as a member of the steering committee in 1972. Compassion compelled me to do something about the racial violence we see in life, as the president of a NAACP branch. I organized and conducted protest activities for justice and equality in Texas. I have always been nonviolently involved in the struggle against oppression, injustice, and the problem of lost African American identity.

We will never do anything until we feel strongly about the violence against people that we see daily. Feelings of compassion are the barometers of our self. When we have feelings of compassion, we become aware of our environment in a way that energizes our total behavior. You must understand that intellect does not make anyone do anything. We can know about the needs of people, but still our knowledge alone will not make us do anything about the needs we know. Until energy ignites knowledge by the energy of feelings, it is static. Moreover, our will is an outward expression of feelings and intellect. When the feelings and intellect get together then our wills make the acts of nonviolent resistance happen. When we act as non-violent resistors, it is our will functioning as the result of our feelings and intellect. This is how we become defenders of the powerless in life. It is not until all four components, thinking, feeling, acting, and physiology, of our total behavior function, that we are able to address the violent issues in life. Your nonviolent resistance is your total behavior facing violent behavior in life. Nonviolent resistance is a local political tool for building community.

Local politics are more important to people than national politics. In local politics, we are closer to the powers that affect us most. Our elected dogcatcher affects us more than the national dog catcher. We need our dogs controlled where we live. National dogs do not affect us too much. The dog next door is the problem that we need to have addressed by the local dog-catcher. This analogy can apply in most political situations. This is where the importance of politics begins. This is true because all politics are local issues. What things cause us the most political problems in life? The answer is the local issues. Distribution is the final act of the political system. You must inform your community about political matters. We need to make sure that the distribution is fair. This is why nonviolent resistance is an important part of Incarnation Centered Spirituality. Nonviolent resistance keeps the political order responsive to all of the people. The tool of nonviolent resistance is necessary for community enlightenment. The community must be enlightened to their constitutional obligation of nonviolent resistance. This right and obligation is clearly stated in the Constitution; American citizens have this right of peaceable assembly. Nonviolent resistance is necessary to protect the ideals expressed in the Constitution. The Constitution of the United States embodies the ideals of human rights. This collection of ideals gives us something for which we must forever be ready to defend, by nonviolent resistance. Ideals are desirable that uplift the race. When we see a desirable ideal, we must work to bring it into action. Once we have achieved the ideal, then it is no longer an ideal, it is a fact. As we achieved the ideal, it became a concrete reality, operating in the community. There is some confusion between the concept of the ideal and the concrete existence of the ideal, as it relates to the application of nonviolent resistance. A constant act of nonviolent resistance is necessary to obtain the concrete reality. When we think that an achieved ideal is no longer an ideal, then the energy goes out of the pursuit. Therefore, the Constitution is a document that sets forth the ideals of a great society for which we must remain in a posture of nonviolent resistance. If we ever reach the point when we think that we have achieved the ideals, we will become conservative and complacent. Perhaps, we no longer use nonviolent resistance to maintain our achievements.

The reality of the Constitution, however, is that we will never reach the ideals that are contained therein. The values are more attainable than the ideals. The ideals, in the Constitution, are such that they can be in direct conflict with the values of mankind. We see this in the fact that the very people who framed the document, ignored ideals in the Constitution and Bill of Rights, such as, freedom, justice, and identity, when these ideals conflicted with their values. The framers of the Constitution and Bill of Rights were slaveholders. From the very beginning, the ideals conflicted with the framers' human values. Ironically, the values in the Constitution fostered the ideal of utopia. The most dangerous ideal in Western thinking is the ideal of utopia. This utopian ideal has perpetrated more violence on the peoples of the world than any other ideal in history. John C. Mohawk states clearly that utopian ideologies lead to justifiable plunder. There is no reason to doubt that people are capable of embracing an imaginary perfect world while pursuing materialistic objectives. In such pursuits, "it is important to note that the utopian vision is the primary goal, while plunder, although unattractive, is a secondary objective."[20] Therefore, law is necessary because of ideals that conflict with values. What makes law necessary is that people have their own ideals that very often conflict with other people's ideals. Law does not have to be fair; it just has to be legal. This is where we find the need for nonviolent resistance. The legality of the law changes when nonviolent resistance demonstrates against it. After all, the Constitution and the Bill of Rights are the main sources of our laws in the United States of America. We will still have to correct and amend laws in order to keep them legal, as evidenced by the unjust illegal Segregation laws in the United States, before the demonstrations of nonviolent resistance in the 1960s' Civil Rights struggles. This has always been the reality of all civilizations throughout history. An excellent example to recall is the need for the Magna Carta of England in 1215, which involved some violence that gave liberties regulating the relationship between King John and his vassals, which later applied to all the people of England. Nevertheless, nonviolent resistance has always been the method to correct violence.

Control is the most important discipline that a person can possess. The truth of the matter is we are always behaving in order to control our environment. Our total behavior, which consists of "the four components: acting, feeling, thinking, and the physiology associated with all our actions, thoughts, and feelings are always acting to control."[21] We use the four components of the total behavior to control our situations. When our control gets out of order, we become very dangerous to ourselves and to others. Provocations can happen that cause us to lose our balance, and then we lose control. Therefore, we must have a nonviolent method to get what we need. When we have lost control, we have also lost the ability to be nonviolent. We must learn to have moderation in all things. When we lose the human ability to make choices intellectually, instead of automatically responding emotionally, we have lost the ability to control our environment in a nonviolent way. What makes this important is the fact that we must always be nonviolent resistors in life. However, if we have lost control, we have lost the very ability to be nonviolent resistors against violent resistors in the world.

Nonviolent resistance is necessary to protect the potential in our children. Human potential is the greatest possibility for positive accomplishments in our world. When we have the potential for certain good things in life, we are a blessing to society. But you must understand that not all potential is for good. Every one of us must be careful teachers of the children. The potential in a child for good is our greatest treasure. We must protect the good potential in children and correct the bad potential in children. Genetics is the best way we have right now, in this time of our history to understand the potential in children this is why we must not be led astray by racism, class bias, or sexism. There is a wealth of treasure in children. We must dig for the wealth, while they are still children. Imagination is the first thing that indicates potential in children. A child at play is an indication of its potential. We are hurting for the kind of potential that works to save the community. It is frightening to learn that our children are lagging behind other nations in academic achievement. This is another reason why nonviolent resistance is necessary. The failure of our children is a waste of our nation's precious treasures. We must develop a strong desire for compassion, as nonviolent resistors, to the under-development of achievement in our children.

Desire, as discussed earlier, is the force that drives most of us. We have a strong need to accomplish, possess, or act, and this desire drives us though life. Sometimes this is good and sometimes this is bad. What matters most is that we understand the power of desire. Compassion must be a component of desire. Compassion is the positive energy that produces good works for the community. When compassion controls and modifies our desires, then we will be a positive force for good. Suffering is the visible sign of violence, while survival is the result of the societal compassion. Society generates nonviolent resistance which is important to the community. When the voice of the masses speaks with the compassion of nonviolent resistance, the system reacts to release the pressure. You must always remember that nonviolent resistance is about the Beloved Community.

The Kingdom of God is a sense of the Beloved Community. It is where the reign of God is present. The rule of the Supreme Being is operating for the good of the whole community. This is the ideal of the Beloved Community. It is in this community where the fellowship of people rests upon the fellowship of the Supreme Being. Enlightenment is more than just a philosophy, it is an expression of an inner sense of the laws of God. It is the way of being in the right relationship with the Creator. God is now the God beyond God. God beyond God is no longer captive in a linguistic symbol. Enlightenment is realizing that God is beyond the human concept of God. The ultimate presence of God is in a nonviolent resistance to a world of oppression. Experiencing the ultimate presence of God is recognizing that even God is held captive in our world, linguistically speaking. The Beloved Community is the Kingdom of God on earth. It is where nonviolent resistance has liberated God from utopian ideals. Acceptance is the last thing that we must do, in the role of a nonviolent resistor. You must recognize that the only way that you can live in this world, as a whole person, is by nonviolent resistance. Nonviolent resistance is a healthy sense of spiritual wholeness.

It lets us view the world through a single-minded vision. Nonviolent resistance is a worldview that is consistent with how Jesus viewed the world. Your worldview will shape your view of money, in the same way, as it shaped Jesus' view. In Chapter 19, you will learn the real spiritual value of money.

Chapter 19

There is More to Money than Spending It

Oh, religion is a fortune, I really do believe,
Oh religion is a fortune, I really do believe,
Oh, religion is a fortune, I really do believe,
Where Sabbaths have no end.

The African American enslaved creators of the above spiritual, "Religion Is a Fortune I Really Do Believe," had come to realize that religion is more valuable than money. They believed religion was the greatest wealth they could acquire. Their faith in God, they believed, was more important than money. However, this is contrary to the thinking of most people. The desire of most people is to acquire money. Most people are driven by the desire to accumulate money and all forms of material wealth. The fact of the matter is that most people have placed their faith in money as their object of security. Howard John Zitko informs us that we have a primitive instinct for survival, which produces a state of fear in us. He suggests that our greatest fear is "the fear of lack."[22] Many people do spend a lifetime trying to overcome this fear by accumulating material wealth represented by money. Many, on the other hand, have overreacted, by turning from all active efforts to gain material wealth as represented by money and instead have decided to live as poverty-stricken people living from hand to mouth and living without material wealth. Both of these attitudes reflect a misunderstanding about the spiritual property of money and material wealth represented by money. Jesus understood the fear of lack that drives most people to worry about their survival. He instructed those who would follow Him not to worry about survival. Jesus says, "Therefore, I say to you, do not worry about your life, what you will eat or what you will drink: nor about your body, what you will put on. Is not life more than food and the body more than clothing [Matthew 6:25]"? Jesus does not say we do not need these things, he says that we do not need to worry about these things. There is a spiritual property about all things especially money.

LEE W. TURNER

The spiritual property of money includes both wealth and capital in their higher spiritual implications. When you discover the spiritual property of money, you will be able to reverse the instinctive fear of lack so prevalent in your mind and replace it with an inner understanding of the nature of abundance. This understanding of the nature of abundance comes with the right attitude toward your acquisition of money. You must understand that money is nothing more or less than scraps of paper, bits of metal, shells, and anything else agreed upon by the people concerned. Understand that the real value of money is not in its natural worth, but in that which it represents. Your challenge is to decide if you will put the value of money in people or in policy. The two types of values of money are the value, which respects the person as the creative worker, or the value, which respects scarcity as a policy. Howard John Zitko sums up this idea of the value of money by saying "If it represents performed services or goods already produced, it is indicative of the natural economic order, that is, a system of value exchange, which respects the rights of the creative worker. If the money, on the other hand, represents bonds or services promised to be performed, it is indicative of a system of value exchange based, not upon creativity as a right, but upon scarcity as a policy."[23]

The world systems carry on business, according to Zitko, with bonded currency, whose value is tied to faith in the government, or tied to faith in multi-national corporations, rather than to the actual worth of human energy and property. This practice is what makes money problematic in the world. Money in itself is not evil. You must understand that money is the medium by which the exchanges of goods and services take place in a society. Moreover, money is the means whereby the end to which it is applied overrides the error of the system, such as when the money is used for the uplifting of the community. The desire to possess money for the sake of money is evil. St. Paul says, "For the love of money is a root of all sorts of evil, and some longing for it have wandered away from the faith, and pierced themselves with many a pang [1Timothy 6:10]." The love of money prevents the community from using money as an instrument for measuring the extent to which it influences the development of those in the community. The goal of the economic life is not to accumulate money for the sake of gaining security, but to spend money for the purpose of transcending the necessity to be concerned about security. By now, you should understand spirituality to mean your development of high moral and cultural achievement arising from unselfish acts to build the community.

Thus, spirituality is your discipline for making the right use of your time, constructively using your energy to build community, and thereby making yourself an authentic person of value. It is a way of life that enables you to use things without having to abuse the things you use. Thus, money is more than something to spend. Moreover, money in the spiritual sense is not for possession as a personal right. Therefore, it is your acceptance of the responsibility for using your physical energies through spiritual channels that you are made fit to become an enlightened worker for the Beloved Community. It is true of you, just as it is true of the singers, of the spiritual mentioned earlier in this chapter. Your attitude toward money, and not money itself, must be your primary concern. All spiritual progress depends on the manner in which you exchange your value with your fellowman, as well as the direction you channel the value within the area of your actions. You must believe that money is a medium of exchange, without value in itself, but representative of human worth, being instituted by man for the moral purpose of fulfilling a spiritual responsibility toward God and man.

Let's Call it Money

As we learned earlier, money does not have to be dollars. It can be shells from the sea. There just needs to be an agreement by members of the society as to its form. The power of money is the ability to make things happen. This power keeps society moving. The ability to purchase goods and services is the idea of money exchange. Your attitude about this exchange is important. You must understand that money creates the possibilities of getting a community to work together. Money is a positive medium of exchange used for the people in the community to feel like they are getting the value of their efforts in whatever they might be doing in the community, as a part of their survival. Money operates under a self-executive law of reciprocity, which means that in the end, you always get back just what you deserve, according to the energy that you used.

Thus, the need for self-worth is the thing that makes money of a community important. Money determines the stability of the economy. Nevertheless, there is more to money than just a piece of material for purchasing goods and services. Money is the symbol of the economic life of the people. We say money does not make the person; the person makes the money. There may be some truth in this statement. The ability to earn money and the way we earn money is the way society measures us, as persons of worth.

The symbol, as it relates to money, is buried treasure. The money that is used is always the money that is in circulation. However, the circulation of money always goes in the cycle of buried and back to the surface. Therefore, work is the energy used to generate this buried treasure. Society buries the treasure in its fundamental nature. In other words, the value of money derives from the amount of digging necessary to bring the buried treasure up buried from the ground of society. When you view money, in the sense of buried treasure, then you will understand the concept of digging. Digging is any form of energy used to bring the treasure from its hiding place. Money in society is underground until it is brought to the top of the ground by your energy. In this sense, energy is money.

Money Has a Divine Quality

Remember creation is an act of divinity. This is why money is always in the divine act of Creation. Work in the context of the divinity of money is also a sacred act. Work is a form of creation that causes things to come into being. Money always follows work because money responds to the creative power of work. Money is a part of this form of creation. As we have seen, money can be in the form of anything. However, there is always some kind of money exchanged for goods and services. Abundance is the natural result of work; it does not have to be any particular kind of work. Work must be a form of creative act that represents God's intentions in Creation. The Creation of God is an ongoing process. God is always creating. Therefore, money is the medium that keeps the process of creation going in the community. Reward is the return for that which makes things better for community. The reward for goods and services is money. Money is the greatest reward a community can give a person. Therefore, money has power. Nevertheless, money is for more than purchasing pleasure for the flesh. Money is power.

Power, as you know, also has the ability to attract. Money is the greatest power for keeping the community in the motion of building a wholeness that is necessary for the welfare of the people of the community. The representation of the wholeness of community is in the money of the community. The community is also able to help its people when the money is circulating. This is why the power of money to attract social improvements represents the level of the living conditions of the people of the community. You must enlighten the community that the solution for most problems in a community comes down to the money of that community. Community, you must remember, is a collection of people working to make their living conditions a healthy and safe way of living. If community is broken then the people are also broken. Therefore, the healthy community instills its faith in the creative ability of the people instead of in the government and multinational corporations. The people who center themselves in God are trustworthy stewards. Your mission is to help the community to understand the economics of stewardship.

Economics, after all, is a process of stewardship.

When the economy of a community is good, then the stewardship of the community is good. There can never be a better economy for a community than its stewardship. When the money is flowing right, stewardship is working in the way to produce equality for the people. The attraction of money is working when there is enough goods and services flowing in an equally, unbiased way. So then, it follows that it is necessary to work for freedom, justice, and identity. Compensation must work along the lines of equality. When there is a fair compensation for the goods and services produced in the community, then a community has learned how to manage money. All money is the constant flow of the people's energy to maintain a healthy environment. Their occupation is for the good of the people. Moreover, the stewardship of money is good for community. In a sense, earning money and stewardship of money are different sides of the same coin.

Your Occupation is Your Treasure

The type of position people have in digging for the buried treasure in the community is occupation. The occupation they have must be compensated by an equal amount of money. The money must be equal to the contribution they make to the welfare of the community. You must teach what keeps the community moving towards improvements that are necessary for a clean and healthy community. Remember that money has the power to make things happen. Things happen because the bottom line is the energy of money. As we learned, acquisition is the natural part of being human. We acquire things because we have a desire for them. The need to acquire things is what keeps the community moving. Energy is the ability to do work. Money is the energy that produces the ends. Money, therefore, is the mean not the end. The means work in more ways than just as the stuff by or in which we acquire things. The means is also the logic of ability. The ability to get what we desire is the reason that money is so important in the world. This is why money is the substance of desire, too. Money gives us the capability to do and have what we can afford. Purchase is the possibility of obtaining what is available. When we purchase a thing, it does not have to be the most necessary thing. It only has to be the available thing we want.

Therefore, the real reason that people purchase anything does not have to be because it is something they must have. Need is definitely more than something to assure our survival. Our wants may be just as necessary to our self-image, which makes them for us at the time our needs. We may want a thing just because we can afford it and in many cases cannot afford it. Nevertheless, we just want it. You must help the community distinguish between their needs and their wants. The behavior of confusing needs with wants can become a money problem. Money becomes the problem when we confuse money with something we only spend. This happens when we have a hard time distinguishing needs from wants. This is why there is also a spirituality of economics. Economics operates on a divine law that makes money necessarily a sacred item. Sacred here does mean an idol god, but rather, an object of respect from God, that operates according to divine law.

There is No Free Lunch According to Divine Law

Divine law requires that there must be something for something. There is no such thing as something for nothing. Divine law operates in all things. In fact, it might be said, that divine law is the Mind of the Creator at work in the Creation causing things to move according to the intention of the Creator. Moreover, this is why you must know what the transfer of knowledge, in the exchange for money means. Understand that if there is no knowledge then the community falls to a level of barely existing as human beings. The universe does not prevent the level of poverty that causes suffering and death of people because of the lack of knowledge. This is why the whole world suffers when people in a far away country die from starvation and other things preventable by knowledge. Ignorance of divine law is not an excuse.

Enlightening the community is your responsibility to the people in the community. There is no reason why anybody should die because of the lack of food, water, or a clean environment. This is why in the end we all suffer until we find a solution for these problems. The only way you can remain a whole person in the Path of the Via Communitiva, is when you are working to enable the people in the community, to become whole people. Building a better community is the way your knowledge is exchanged for the money that works for a better community. Moreover, this knowledge is about how to keep money flowing for the development of community. Knowing how to use the blessings of money for the betterment of people is benevolence.

The blessing of money is revealed in the knowledge of benevolence. When you are in the spirit of benevolence, you are in the flow of knowing the blessings of money. You must understand that money is not that which you just accumulate for your own personal good. Moreover, you attract money because you are in the spirit of benevolence. Thus, while thrift is the act of saving money nevertheless it is also the act of giving money away. When we get money in order to give it away, then we have learned the meaning of money as a blessing to the community. The Apostle Paul says, "Let him that stole steal no longer; but rather let him labor, working with his hands the thing which is good, that he may have to give to him that needeth [Ephesians 4:28]." The main purpose of money is the ability to accumulate it in order to put it to work for the good of other people. The rich man, in the story of Lazarus, did not go to hell because he was rich. He went to hell because he did not use his riches to help Lazarus get rich. Your destiny is in knowing the meaning of knowledge as the blessing of money. Money is the result of knowledge and knowledge is the result of money. An idle mind is void of wealth and needs instruction in the stewardship of accumulating money for the purpose of giving it away to enhance the community.

Economics is Stewardship of Creation

Economics is the stewardship of the household of the Creator. As pointed out earlier, stewardship is about money; it is also about the Creation. The earth belongs to God. Additionally, the person who takes care of the earth, as if it belongs to God, will always practice wholesome economics. The economics practiced must consider other people in the world who need help to survive. It is the purpose of the Creator for the rich to help the poor. However, the most twisted concept about Creation is the concept of rich and poor. We must share the goods of the Creation. Goods are part of the economy that operates on the law of the medium of exchange. We get the value of our goods according to the energy we apply. The goods could be anything used for the exchange for money. The goods will always have an intrinsic and an extrinsic value. We take both of the values in consideration when we exchange goods for money. Both are the overall value we receive in money. There is no use trying to exchange a rag for riches unless the rag has the intrinsic and extrinsic values that you are asking for. Services operate in the same way. We receive pay for the value of services we render according to the energy we used in performing the service. The value of service performed is derived from what it does to help people achieve wholeness. The need for our wholeness is the unseen force that makes a thing valuable. Labor is different from service, in the degree, that it requires the person's physical energy. Your labor operates in reverse order. It does not matter how much physical energy is used what matters is what happens on the other end of the energy spent. It may not take more time or energy than just pushing a button. Nevertheless, the value is in what it does for people on the other end of the button. This is what it means to understand the medium of exchange. It is important to know that time is as important as the energy spent in producing goods and services. Time is worth its salt in gold.

Time is Money

There is a time factor in money. The time factor in money is the duration it takes to generate the amount of money made. When the time is equivalent to the money received, then there has been a fair exchange. Where are the long days of work for the small amount of pay gone? It has gone by way of the child labor law and other human rights laws. Nevertheless, there are still those who think they are taking advantage of people in under-developed nations by long work hours and very little pay. This is just a reminder that there is no such thing as something for nothing. Creation does not operate this way. It causes a breakdown in the system of the created order when there is disregard for the time and money factor in society. Time is money. We waste money, the same way, we waste time. When you fail to manage your time, chances are you fail to manage your money. When you give time the same value that you give money, then you understand the time factor of money. Reciprocity is the process of equal return. The return for effort spent doing what you do will always be in direct proportion to the time, energy, and money factor. It takes as long to do something in an hour as it does to do the same thing in fifteen minutes. The law of reciprocity finally catches up with the person who has not learned this relationship between time, energy, and money. Compensation, as we have pointed out, also operates under divine law.

Compensation is, also, a divine quality of money. Compensation is the way money reflects its divinity. This built in factor in the Creation is expressed as sowing and reaping. This is the law of compensation. There is a payoff for whatever we do. This is also true of how we honor God with money. The scripture expresses this fact of honoring God with His money as tithes. Malachi 3:10 says, "Bring all the tithes into the storehouse, that there may be food in my house, and try Me now in this... if I will not open for you the windows of heaven and pour out for you such blessings that there will not be room enough to receive it." This is what we mean when we say money makes money. A tithe is an investment in God. Investment is the process we use as the act of sowing money. When we invest money in something, we expect to receive a harvest--a return. The greatest investment we can make is in the creative force of God. Force is also a trait of divinity. This is why money is a symbol of divinity. It has controlling force. This is why we expect our money to do what we want it to do. The force of money is so strong that it causes war when it is out of control. War comes from the desire for money in order to do what we want to do for our own pleasures. The Scripture says, "You lust and do not have; so you commit murder. And you are envious and cannot obtain; so you fight and quarrel. You do not have because you do not ask [James 4:2]." Spiritual power controls force. The spiritual power of money is just as real as the physical power of war. Money can cause the person who values money for money's sake to become a miser and worshiper of money. This is not what you ought to do. Therefore, there is a built in defense system called idolatry. Money is of God and God knows its power so this is why God made the worship of money a sin. Life is the most sacred possession in Creation. Therefore, money must respect and reserve the sacred nature of life.

Life is sacred. Therefore, everything that helps to make life whole is sacred. For this reason, God created money as a sacred object. Money can cause abusive behavior from those who approach money from the negative side of greed. Having the wrong understanding of money is very dangerous. You must never forget that money is a sacred object. Instead, you must always remember that it represents the goodness of God. This is why, in the early days of human history, banks were always located in the temples. Money is a sacred object. There was also a time in this country when people entered banks in a reverent, silent, respectful way. It was not until we made money a secular object of pleasure that we started to view money as an object of selfish indulgence. The best way to describe banks today is as regulatory agencies. Banks regulate the money of the world. This is why there is so much brokenness in the world. Blessings will flow to the poor people of the world once again, when we learn that there is a divine quality about money. Moreover, money demands the same kind of respect that we give the Creator. This is not a suggestion that you must worship money, but it is a reminder that you must respect money as an object for wholeness in a broken world, and that it is to be used as an object for healing. Money should be brought to the Beloved Community. In Chapter 20, you will learn about the Beloved Community and why money is so important to its development.

Chapter 20

Living Your Own Life on the Journey

Walk together children, don't you get weary,
Walk together children, don't you get weary,
Oh, talk together children, don't you get weary,
There's a great camp meeting in the promised
Land.

The enslaved singers of this spiritual, "Walk Together Children," knew that there is a positive unified destiny at the end of the journey. They called it the "Promised Land." Many of us know that God is the all-knowing Creator. God knows all there is to be known about the Creation. Your knowledge of God is God's knowledge of you. The more you know of God, the more you know of yourself. You can know nothing of God outside of God, except through the revelation of God. You can know your unified destiny because Almighty God knows the meaning of your journey to the Promised Land. Your ability to make the journey is in the control of God. This is why you put your journey in the hands of God by your complete obedience to God. When you let God take the lead in your journey, then you made your journey with the best of ease. This is the purpose of letting God lead you in your journey. This is an important concept. Hearing and applying the concept of letting God lead you in your journey, has its purpose; you must understand how important obedience is to your journey. Your obedience to God's Word led you into your journey. And it is the obedience to God's Word that will sustain you in your journey. Obedience is both a quantifier and a qualifier in the spiritual journey. Your obedience informs you of the right path, as well as, measures your depth of spiritual growth on the path. You needed to know that the purpose for serving the Beloved Community is the most important thing about your journey. Now that you are in the Beloved Community, you still need to rely on God through your obedience to God's Word. God knows the purpose of your journey, and guides you in order to help you serve the community. Each of us has a different purpose of service in the journey of life. You can see why the journey must always be in the hands of God. We take the journey of wholeness, in the first place, to learn how to trust God in the Beloved Community. The technique of Enlightenment on the Path of the Via Communitiva makes us aware of trusting God in our historical environment.

We Live in an Historical Environment

We live in an historical environment that shapes our journey for living in the Beloved Community in the context of history. The historical environment is the ideas, ideologies, traditions, and other attitudes, value systems and belief systems surrounding your life at all times. This is why you had to learn that the journey is not your journey alone. The environment had a great deal to do with the journey in order to get you ready to serve the Beloved Community. In fact, the environment had a lot to do with what called you into the journey in the first place. The expectations that we bring to the journey have a great deal to do with what our conditions are in our surroundings.

History is the context that defines your journey. You can never operate outside of history. It does not matter what the times may be in which you are operating and working; history will have as much to do with the journey, as it will have to do with serving the community. You must realize that you are a historical being. You are historical because you must reflect on the past. Humans live within a stream of time, flowing in a finite world, in which the only constant is change. We always hear the Word of God within a historical context. We can only know God in our historical context, as He is to us historical creatures, because God Himself is infinite and unknowable. For this reason, the Christian spiritual masters can talk of the spiritual in such different ways.

We are born with the ability to use language. However, history itself presents a language problem for us. This problem of language is vital, because we are our language. Moreover, language is historical as well. We come to the world into an environment with the ability to develop the language of the environment. However, historical and physical environment shape the language we develop. This is true because language changes in time and in different environments. Consider the language of the preamble of the Declaration of Independence. In the historical period of 1776, and in the environment of White landholders and slaveholders, the language had a different meaning for enslaved African men and women. The language, "We hold these truths" has always been problematic in the United States of America when applied to non-Europeans. The struggle for liberty, justice, and identity today in America, still consists of trying to get the language of the Declaration of Independence, printed in 1776, to include all Americans. This is your community service. You are born with a unique set of codes for the journey to the Beloved Community as a whole person. You must follow the codes you bring into the world in order to follow them in your service to the community. God draws you to your path through your codes. The Christian spiritual masters, throughout the centuries, have described this process of one being drawn into the journey of life, as journey into the unknown. We are incomplete humans until we yield to the drawing power of the Holy Spirit and, until we enter onto the path of wholeness to become servants of the Beloved Community. God knew your path of service before you ever came into the world.

The foreknowledge of God is the initial start of your journey. God knows what you are to do in life. You need to understand, that for God to know, is for God to do that which God knows. Knowing and doing with God are the same. God assigns the roles we play in life before we are born, or we may take roles on our self, after we are born. The roles we take on our self, will never take us to where God wants us to go. We must live the roles that God assigned us if we want to become whole servants in this broken world. The role that God has assigned you is your journey. Your journey is the race that God has sent you into the world to run. You will never realize your true meaning in life, if you do not take on your role that God has assigned. Even though, human beings are born broken persons because of sin, God puts in our soul a desire for wholeness. This desire is in the very core of our being.

The Divine Life Force is in the Core of Your Soul

The core is that place in the soul where the divine life force is located. It is the center of the soul. We are seeking the root of wholeness in life. This root is where God talks to you about your journey of wholeness for your service to the community. This is your prayer in life. Prayer is a contextual relationship grounded in your expectations that God speaks to you and that you can hear God speak. This expectation is what we mean by faith. Therefore, it is in your core, where you first learn about your journey. Unfolding from the core is, in fact, the journey you are taking in life. If your journey is flowing from your core then it is flowing from God. All things flow from God and back to God through the inner core of our souls. The soul is the part of the self that must deal with our journey; it is the first part of the self that gets the message of our journey in life. Our development is the real reason for the journey. You must understand that the real purpose of the journey is your unique development. You must develop into the person you entered into the world to become. Ultimately, your development will help others in the community to develop. The ultimate purpose for your development is community development. The developed community is here to help others to develop. Therefore, wholeness in the community is first a self-development project. When the self is whole, then it can work towards the wholeness of community.

Your uniqueness is the purpose of your journey. It is on the journey that we discover that there is no other person in the world exactly like another person. Our uniqueness, in the world, is the reason for personal responsibility. It is the responsibility of the individual to be who the individual comes into the world to become. When this does not happen, then the individual must take the responsibility for failing to develop. Your development depends on your prayer life. Being in tune to God is the real meaning of hearing the music of God playing just for you. You hear your own music because you have your own rhythm; nobody else can hear your music. You see we are marching in life to our unique rhythm. This is why the insight of rhythm is personal. Directions come in rhythmic beats that nobody can hear, but the person for whom it is intended. This makes the insight of the individual important. Each spirit-filled rhythm is part of the great symphony of community. This is what the enslaved singers of the "Walk Together Children," spiritual meant by Promised Land.

Discovering community is your mission in life. This discovery is exciting. Being aware of learning makes learning fun. Discovery of community is the greatest event that can happen on your journey. The enslaved singers, of the last spiritual learned that walking together led to the great Camp Meeting in the Promised Land. The purpose of your journey is to discover the wonders in Creation that lead to community. The most exciting knowledge that you can discover on your journey is the foundation of community. You do not have to create community, you only have to discover it. This is why saints are the most useful persons in the community. The saint who makes the journey to wholeness has made the hero's venture and has come back into the community to teach survival skills to the people of the community. The adventure is your calling to make the journey to wholeness. Your journey is full of unpredictable experiences that you will have to overcome through personal discipline. When you overcome the unpredictable events, you learn a valuable lesson for the community. The promise of wholeness becomes apparent. Moreover, it becomes apparent that it is important for you as an African American community to develop alternative expressions of thinking, seeing, and being, in a racially oppressed society. Therefore, the returning saint must teach the community the importance of learning how to interpret, confront, embrace, and transcend current oppressive realities. By saints, we mean heroes. The hero makes a physical journey into the unknown; the saints make a spiritual journey into the unknown. Christian Spirituality is an inward journey to discover wisdom for transforming yourself and your community. Remember, when you are in this path of wholeness, you are taking a journey for the good of the whole community. This is what makes learning fun. By watching carefully, you will begin to see patterns in life, that belong to the wholeness of community. You will also be able to see the patterns better in the community because you will have learned to see them better in your personal life. We learn to desire the Beloved Community just as Rev. Dr. Martin L. King, Jr. and other African American spiritual masters have done since 1619 A.D.

Your DNA Codes Are Really for Your Survival

As we have seen, the DNA in our genes makes us aware of the journey, which we must take in life. For this to occur, it is necessary for your soul to unfold from within. The soul is the receiving station for the messages that come from the environment to wake up the codes in our genes. The codes we brought into the world are within us to make our journey in life. Our journey is for our service to the community. Your sensitivity is clearly more than just for responding to physical stimuli. It is the built in precondition to make you alert to the messages coming to you through the environment and from your Creator. Your response, if you are obedient, is the path you are following. This path is the trail you followed until you reach wholeness for serving your community. When you were on the path that you are supposed to be on you meet the necessary things and people you need for your journey. This is why you must see the trends in your life to stay alert to life.

The trend is that which is happening in your vision. When you see the vision, then a trend will appear to you. The vision is what is taking place in a general way. You did not make the vision. When there is a vision, a trend also follows that vision. When we discover the trend and vision, then we can develop our own niche. The niche is that which we have developed for the trend we see. The vision now is the search of humanity, a search for a new relationship with the Creator. The trend in the world is the aspiration to move into a real relationship with the Creator in every household. This trend will help you to develop your niche. When we read the daily news and listen to the television, we learn that there is a great deal of confusion in the world. It seems as if humanity has lost hope in the systems of man. This vision informs you in your journey. Your journey is your hope. Similarly, your anticipation works along with your vision and the trend as a part of your niche. You alone must develop your niche according to the trend.

It's All in the Trends

Following a trend will give shape to your journey. However, we follow the trend with our own niche. This niche is the activity of your community. The trend we follow is the production of our wholeness, along the five-fold path of Incarnation Centered Spirituality. Incarnation Centered Spirituality: the five-fold path to wholeness is the trend. The Turner E.A.G.L.E. Technique for achieving wholeness in a broken world will lead you to wholeness along this five-fold path. The Turner E.A.G.L.E. Technique is the niche. It is just one way to participate in the trend of African Americans returning to their spiritual ancestry. They are returning for the empowerment of their own soul. They are seeking empowerment for soul survival in a complex system of racism, discrimination, and dehumanization. Wholeness is what most of us are looking for.

Personal wholeness is the light at the end of the tunnel. The light comes in the darkness, when there is a spark of fire. In the journey to wholeness, this spark of fire is the light that illuminates the path on which we travel. Current times have collapsed into an insecurity that comes in cycles in human history. The trends we see in the world shape our life. The trend that most people have taken is the path that they think will help to give them wholeness. However, this is unrealistic. Trends do not give us wholeness. What matters is what we do with the trends. Thus, we develop our own niche in the trends, our own spiritual discipline.

We can design our niche for what we expect in life. Therefore, expectations are always along the lines of what we have developed for the self. We African Americans must work for the Beloved Community as whole persons. Only we know what the Beloved Community looks like in our history. The path of our niche will take us to the wholeness that we need for building the Beloved Community. God uses your niche as the pulling power in the world that operates to draw us to our terminal goal of wholeness in the Beloved Community. We have the responsibility to take the path. Nevertheless, even if we do not decide to take the path, the path will continue to pull on us. Our struggle in life will be the struggle between where we want to be and where we are supposed to be. There will be no peace in your life until you decide to take the path that was designed for you, even before your birth. The path to wholeness that you take does not have to be Incarnation Centered Spirituality, but it will be a version of it. It will always be the path of Jesus Christ. It does not matter what we call it. Nevertheless, it flows from the Incarnation. The Turner E.A.G.L.E. Technique for Incarnation Centered Spirituality is the spiritual discipline that brings fulfillment, when followed to the terminal goal of wholeness in life while serving the Beloved Community, without which there is no sense of fulfillment. Your journey in life will always be your niche. Your niche is your fire in life for the Beloved Community.

Light Your Own Fire with Your Touch

Ignite your fire in life by developing your niche! You can do this with just your touch. You have more power than you realize. Your touch makes the difference. When the hand, which is part of the central force of Creation, touches something, it comes to life. We transform things for better or worse in Creation with our touch. Your transformation brings transformation to your environment. You must teach this concept to the community. The touch of powerful individuals throughout history has changed the world. The greatest touch throughout history is the touch of Jesus. It is our responsibility to follow Jesus in his touch of redemption for the Beloved Community. It is the work of redemption that Incarnation Centered Spirituality: The Five-fold Path to Wholeness produces. Support comes from heaven when we are in the path of redemption for the Beloved Community. Your touch in life makes the difference because you have the divine touch. The Beloved Community is the celebration of the victory of the divine touch. Your mission is to teach the community how to celebrate this victory.

Community is the Dance of Victory

Celebration is the acknowledgement of the victory in life that we anticipated. When we celebrate, it is like a dance around a victory pole. This is why the journey is a dance down a starlit path to wholeness. The celebration comprises the journey. This is why the journey is a shouting dance. Community is the place of celebration. It is a dance of victory in Jesus. We make the declaration by the celebration that we have overcome a great fight with the satanic forces in life. And with Jesus, we have been victorious. We become whole in the battle and we become wiser from the battle. How can we have wholeness in any other way? We learn, in the journey, that life is more than clothes and food and material things. Life is the path that we take which leads to victory. Embracing the Incarnation is the same as embracing life. It is not just any life, but the life that Jesus brought to this world when he was born in a stable. We dance down a fire lit trail that leads to the wholeness of life for educating the community about African American Spirituality. You must pay your dues for being offspring of African Americans.

Dues are something that we all must pay. We cannot live in this world without paying our dues. When we live in life without paying, we are a deadbeat people. What makes being a deadbeat person so ineffective in life is that they do not have anything to give back to life. We are all supposed to be productive in life. This production is for the community. When we think about it, we realize that we are all indebted to others who made life easier for us. Being free is much better than being chattel property. We can all testify to this fact. This is what makes us call those who struggled for freedom, justice and identity saints in our world. When people make our neighborhoods better in a significant way, we call them heroes but when this contribution is in the name of Jesus, we call them *saints*. The saints in our world are the ones, who just strive from day to day to make things better, without ever asking for anything in return. Free labor is not something that most people like to do. Nevertheless, the volunteer who goes to work and punches a clock just as if being paid is a saint. They are paying their dues. When we pay our dues others always recognize it. Only those with personal wholeness can understand this fact. Wholeness comes with the life that is able to pay its dues. Incarnation Centered Spirituality is the path to wholeness because it brings wholeness to the community as dues paying. The celebration of community is the dance of victory. It is contentment in life.

Contentment in life comes when we realize that a good death is a reward in life. When we realize that death is inevitable, then we realize that the whole trip in life is for the goal of a good death. This is what the singers of the Negro spiritual meant when they said, "I want to die easy when I die, and shout salvation as I fly." Old enslaved saints understood that a good death is a reward in life. We want to die easy when we die. A good death is the reward of the journey. Incarnation Centered Spirituality makes your death worthwhile. The truth in life is that there is nothing in life but nothingness. This knowledge of nothingness is the beginning of understanding the meaning of the Scripture that says, "You brought nothing into this world and it is certain that you can carry nothing out." We must become aware of our own nothingness. What makes us something is the Word of God. God's Word spoke us into being. God's Word keeps us in the state of being. Without the Word of God, we would go back to nothingness. Satisfaction comes when we realize that God's Word keeps us whole through eternity. Your total satisfaction comes when you realize that a good death is a reward in your journey. This is the answer to the riddle of living. We find contentment in this answer to life's problems --live for God's promise of the great camp meeting in the Promised Land.

Your Answer to Life's Problems is in Living Your Life

Solutions and answers to problems always make us content. We cannot rest until we find the correct answer. Moreover, when we find the answer we also find contentment. This is the real goal in life. A life of contentment is a life that has found the answer to the problems in life. The terminal goals are always the reason for your journey. The terminal goal in Incarnation Centered Spirituality is wholeness in the Beloved Community. This is the reason why we took the trip in the first place. Our vision was and continues to be developing the discipline of Incarnation Centered Spirituality. The trend is that African Americans are trying to find personal wholeness in a system of White supremacy. The niche is the Turner E.A.G.L.E. Technique. Furthermore, the niche leads to the Beloved Community. The Beloved Community is the basis of our wholeness. We find that the wholeness in our vision led to the terminal goal. The sense of completion is the most significant thing in life. Completeness is a significant part of life because the broken soul cannot find completeness in a broken world. However, divinity always desires completeness; thereby, leading to wholeness in the Beloved Community. This is what our African American ancestors meant, as they sang the Negro spiritual "Walk Together Children." In this spiritual, they sang, "There's a great camp meeting in the promised land." And so there is.

ENDNOTES

1. Urban T. Holmes, A History of Christian Spirituality: An Analytical Introduction, (San Francisco, Harper & Row, 1980), 11.

2. F. C. Happold, A Journey Inward, (Atlanta: John Knox Press, 1993), 71.

3. William Glasser, Choice Theory: A New Psychology of Personal Freedom, (New York, NY: Harper Collins, 1998), 72.

4. Howard Thurman, The Search for Common Ground: An Inquiry Into the Basis of Man's Experience of Community, (San Francisco, Harper & Row, Pub., 1971), 9.

5. Eric Butterworth, The Concentric Perspective: What's In It From Me? (Missouri: Unity Books, 1989), 2.

6. Henry Drummond, Natural Law In The Spiritual World, (Philadelphia: Henry Altermus Pub., 1883), 10.

7. Arthur Chandler, ARA CCELL: An Essay in Mystical Theology, (London: Methuen and LTD, 1912), 4.

8. Pere Garrigou-Lagrange, The Three ways of the Spiritual Life, (Illinois: Tan Books and Publishers, Inc. 1977), 5.

9. St John of The Cross, Ascent of Mount Carmel, Trans. Ed, E. Allison Peers,(New York, Image Books, 1958), 19.

10. Ibid, 23.

11. F. C. Happold, A Journey Inward, (Atlanta: John Knox Press, 1993), 45.

12. Ibid, 60.

13. Mouni Sadhu, Concentration: A Guide To mental Mastery, (California: Melvin Powers Publisher, 1958), 15.

14. Rowan Williams, Teresa of Avila, (Wilton, CT: Morehouse Publishing, 1999), 116.

15. Arthur Chandler, ARA CCELI: An Essay in Mystical Theology, (London: Methuen and LTD, 1912), 4.

16. William Glasser, M. D., Choice Theory: A New Psychology of Personal Freedom, (New York, NY: Harper Collins Publishers, 1998), 45.

17. Ibid, 92.

18. Urban T. Holmes, A History of Christian Spirituality: An Analytical Introduction, (San Francisco: Harper &Row, 1980), 15.

19. Michael N. Nagler, The Search For A Nonviolent Future: A Promise of Peace for Ourselves, Our Families, and Our World, (San Francisco: Inner Ocean Publishing, 2004), 160.

20. John C. Mohawk, Utopian Legacies: A History of Conquest and Oppression in the Western World, (New Mexico, Clear Light Publishers, 2000), 3.

21. William Glasser, Choice Theory: A New Psychology of Personal Freedom, (New York, NY: Harper Collins, 1998), 72.

22. Howard John Zitko, The Original Lemurian Theo-Christic Conception, (Benson, Arizona: World University Press, 2003), 35.

23. Ibid, 36.

AUTHOR
DR. LEE W. TURNER

It is my great joy to present my first book to my
colleagues, friends, and my readers. I have written
this spiritual self- help book to assist others in im-
proving their life's journey for spiritual wholeness.
Why remain a broken person in a broken world when
one can become a complete whole person
through a spiritual discipline that leads to wholeness in
the context of Christian theology.

Order Information

Additional Books may be ordered from:

Trafford Publishing
2657 Wilfert Road
Victoria, BC, Canada V98 5Z3
Phone: Toll-free 1 888-232-4444
website: www.@trafford.com
Email: info@trafford.com

Supplementary Materials:

Item(s)	Prices
Study Guides	5.00
Study Workbook	25.00
CD	12.97
DVD	13.30
Tape Set (10 tapes)	66.30
Shipping	(not included)

Prices are Subject to Change

Speaking Engagements:

Dr. Lee W. Turner is available for course teaching and speaking engagements, as well as, conference presentations. You may contact the author at:

Pastor Lee W. Turner, Th.D.
Greater New Mount Zion
Missionary Baptist Church
P.O. Box V
207 Eggar Street
Waxahachie, TX 75165
Church: 972 937-4615
Home: 214 943-4940

You may also order signed copies of *The Turner E.A.G.LE. Technique For Incarnation Centered Spirituality* directly from the author.

ORDER FORM

Mail to: Pastor Lee W. Turner
1246 S. Marsalis Avenue, Dallas, TX 75216
214 943-4940

Items	Quantity	Unit Cost	Total Cost	Special Instructions/ Questions
The Turner E.A.G.L.E. Technique ... Book		$25.00		✹ Autographed
Study Guides		$ 5.00		
Study Workbook		$25.00		
CD (Single Lesson)		$12.97		
DVD (Single Lesson)		$13.30		
Tape Set (10 tape set) (Ten Lessons)		$66.30		
Shipping		Not included (Additional Cost)		
Taxes		As Required by Law		
Total*		*Prices are subject to change.		

Name _____ Phone: _____

Address _____

For Office Use Only

Date Received: _____ Date Mailed: _____

Date Completed: _____ Completed By: _____

Glossary

Beloved Community
The Kingdom of God where the believers are working to bring freedom, justice, and identity for the glory of God.

Contemplation
A prayer life of constantly communicating with God.

Sacramentalism
A life of commitment, that leads to a life of consecration to God for the duty of living as Jesus taught his disciples.

Via Communitiva
The way of affirming, striving for the possibility of shared living under the authority of God.

Via Creativa
The way of affirming the creation of God by generating new ideas and artistic ways of serving God and humanity.

Via Negativa
The way of letting go of negative, harmful emotions.

Via Positiva
The way or path of affirming and embracing the Incarnation of Jesus.